NOT FOR
ATTRIBUTION

NOT FOR ATTRIBUTION

*A Treasury of Public Relations/
Public Affairs Anecdotes*

Jon. L. Allen

Library of Congress Number: 99-91546
ISBN #:   Hardcover   0-7388-0870-9
                 Softcover   0-7388-0871-7

This book was printed in the United States of America.

To order additional copies of this book, contact:
Xlibris Corporation
1-888-7-XLIBRIS
www.Xlibris.com
Orders@Xlibris.com

CONTENTS

This book is dedicated with deep respect and affection to the late Rear Admiral Harold Blaine "Min" Miller who enticed me to abandon journalism for a career in corporate public relations. Anyone who ever worked for "Min" or knew him will always remember that the definition of "an officer and gentleman" can only be measured by the standards he set.

FOREWORD

Who doesn't enjoy a good story? And who can resist some anecdotes illuminating the lighter side of an otherwise workaday world?

It's a popular genre. Most libraries contain a wide range of
titles . . . books of legal, political, literary, medical, baseball, military and movie anecdotes. In fact, the catalogue in my excellent
local library contains a total of 63 titles under the heading. And,
while they are yet to be published, there are undoubtedly numerous good stories for virtually every profession or occupation.

Public relations and public affairs are no exception. The very
nature of the work insures that professionals have experienced
amusing, ironic or surprising situations during their careers.

Public relations and public affairs professionals speak to the
press on behalf of their employers or clients. They arrange annual
meetings, product demonstrations, news conferences and special
events. They write speeches. They edit annual reports, publish
magazines and newsletters and produce films and news clips. There
are obviously plenty of opportunities for mistakes, mishaps and
misunderstandings.

During almost 30 years in corporate public relations and government public affairs, I received my share of unreasonable requests and surprises. With a typewriter always close at hand, I
started a modest collection of anecdotes for the amusement of my
colleagues. Then, some of them started sharing a few of theirs with
me.

It was easy to conclude there must be hundreds of additional
anecdotes. So, although I hadn't written a book for 15 years, I
determined to ask active and retired fellow professionals to recol-
lect their favorites.

Assembling and editing a collection of public relations and public affairs anecdotes has, of course, resulted in some pleasant surprises and a few disappointments.

Among the former have been the many supportive letters I've received. Whether contributors were able to provide only one story or as many as half a dozen, they invariably recognized just how entertaining and, even instructive, such a volume would be.

On the other hand, I'm surprised by the number of respondents who claimed nothing amusing happened during the course of long, distinguished careers. Frankly, I can't believe this. I prefer to think circumstances and situations occurred which, in retrospect, were highly amusing but didn't seem so at the time and were best forgotten.

A minor disappointment was the scanty response from academe. Few anecdotes came from educators. This surprised me, because although I've never taught public relations at college level, it would seem useful to collect some good stories for classroom use. Anecdotes are often a helpful way to make a point and prepare future professionals for some surprises.

During the course of reviewing initial contributions, it became apparent it was necessary to set some ground rules, even if it meant leaving out some amusing anecdotes.

The first of these was that the collection of public relations and public affairs anecdotes must concentrate on stories about professionals performing their regular duties. This eliminated several dozen "celebrity" anecdotes in which the public relations practitioner was peripheral.

Also, it was necessary to reject some amusing anecdotes from the world or work simply because there was no professional connection. They were incidents which might just as well have happened to an attorney, an accountant or the proverbial traveling salesman.

Third, the anecdotes had to be true. This eliminated jokes, daffy definitions and one-liners.

Next was a difficult decision regarding the use of actual names.

I consulted several fellow professionals on this point, and they agreed it did not seem necessary. Most readers would not know who the chief executive officer of, say, Worldwide Wickets, Inc., was from 1964 to 1971. The fact he was an unreasonable taskmaster would suffice, since he was by no means alone in that regard. Readers will recognize the type.

Lastly, I've not included any of the numerous stories about something that was supposed to happen, but did not. We've all suffered disappointments, such as the cover story which never ran because of the election of a new pope, a hurricane coming ashore the same week or the press conference which was poorly attended because the city's mayor had just suffered a fatal heart attack.

Public relations and public affairs professionals frequently find themselves in situations in which they can observe human nature at its best or at its worst. While other executives often learn from their mistakes, sometimes at considerable expense, they seldom have to face the fury of a business leader who believes he's been misquoted when, in all likelihood, he wasn't.

As was the original intent, this collection has turned out to be an entertaining project. I hope readers will find many a smile in its pages as they recognize situations which have occurred to others. For those new to our profession or planning to enter it remember: Don't be surprised. Surprises come with the territory.

Jon L. Allen
October, 1999

ACKNOWLEDGEMENTS

Collecting public relations and public affairs anecdotes is somewhat like chasing butterflies. There are some beauties out there, but capturing them can be surprisingly difficult.

This collection of some 200 amusing and true stories contains no footnotes, nor a bibliography. The few books about the profession which are not texts are, for the most part, personal memoirs and not very useful sources. Unlike other collections of anecdotes, this volume could not be researched in existing literature.

I knew I was on the right track when I asked the Information Center at the Public Relations Society of America if they had anything on file under "humor." The response I received from the ever-helpful Amy Goldfarb was a resounding negative.

It's been necessary, therefore, to ask numerous active and retired professionals for their recollections. The response has been great fun. We're deeply indebted to dozens of contributors for sharing their favorite stories.

The anecdotes in this volume were contributed by the following professionals, to whom we here express our profound appreciation: Ralph C. Darrow, Andrew J. Tobin, George Hammond, Barney Oldfield, Candace Greene, Michael W.R. Davis, James R. Ashlock, Eugene Ingold, Max Hampton, Russell R. Pate, Agenor L. Castro, Charles Russhon, Edward Gottlieb, Tim Colwell, Dean S. Sims, Warren H. Goodman, Sally I. Evans, Sloan Auchincloss, Julian Wise, Fraser P. Seitel, John F. Budd, Jr., Michael J. Porter, Ron Gossen, James Battersby, Paul L. Renfrow, William R. Cox, Alan Jasper, Brad Dressler, Arnold Saks, Theodore Lustig, Aaron D. Cushman, John F. Heinz, Anthony M. Franco, Carl M. Cleveland and Betty Vaughn.

Also, Gary Beals, Robert J. Wood, Joseph K. Arimond, Robert E. Rayfield, Denny Griswold, Lloyd N. Newman, Rex H. Blakey, Philip Lesly, Stephen J. Crews, Donald A. Mounce, Robert W. Armstrong, Wolfram J. Dochtermann, William J. Murray, Richard G. Logan, W. Roger Davis, Henry C. Rogers, David L. Jensen, Wilbur Cross, Skip Ragland, Richard E. Williamson, Richard A. Coccola, Stephen J. Allen, Woody Kepner, Anne M. Deschene, Arnold T. Koch, Jr., Henry C. Cranford, Dan P. Millar, N. Richard Lewis, Richard Clark, Harold B. Miller, Frederick Beck, Curtis G. Linke, James E. Hunt and James F. Fox.

And, Leon Tex Taylor, James W. Chandler, David C. Frailey, John W. Walton, S. Wayne Pennington, Charles G. Francis, Patrick J. Cullen, Linda E. Roth, Parker Monroe, James R. Compton, Donald L. Gilleland, A. Bruce Pozzi, Ed Greif, Melvin D. Barger, Milton E. Mitler, Diana Graham, Robert Levinson, G. William Gray, Patrick C.G. Coulter, James J. Richard, Albert E. Kaff, Donald E. Wick, Richard Maney, Julian S. Stein, Jr., Neil T. Regan, Kathy Keenan, Warren A. Logelin, Robert Wigginton, Robert E. Moreillon, Larry Marshall, Ted B. Sherwin, Saul Richman, John H. Murphy, Ed Reed, Charles R. Werle, and Michael J. McDermott.

And, Scott Regan, David L. Sturges, Eileen Milling, Lynne D. Williams, Alan Scott, Kenneth F. Smith, Richard L. Moore, Gene Secunda, Albert Walker, William A. Simpson, Robert G. McCullough, Marshall B. Sitrin, Ray Stahl, Howard Sigmond and Burns W. Lee.

Special thanks to Liz Alexander who converted my manuscript on her computer to a publication-ready format. Liz guided me through an unfamiliar process with patience, optimism and unfailing good cheer.

CAREER COUNSELING

A story the chairman of the board of a leading independent oil company relished telling about himself was a particular favorite whenever he welcomed participants to the company's annual world-wide public relations conference.

It seems that when he entered the University of Texas at Austin, his freshman counselor summoned him for a meeting regarding his academic plans.

"You'd better not plan to major in journalism," the advisor urged. "Frankly, based on your qualifications, you'll have difficulty handling it."

He recommended the young freshman major in something less demanding and suggested geology.

"Best piece of advice I ever received," the chairman loved to conclude. "If I'd been just a bit smarter when I was young, I wouldn't be where I am today."

83-ALLE

PROOF POSITIVE

The public relations director of an oilfield services company in Oklahoma had only two weeks to produce a four-color brochure in Chinese for use at the Canton Trade Fair.

The text was written and approved in haste, color transparencies were separated locally and a Chinese translator and typesetter worked overtime on the project.

To save time and reduce shipping costs, a printer in Singapore was selected to run the job. Film for the brochure and the color separations were sent by courier to the company's division manager in Singapore, together with a blueline to indicate how the pages and the illustrations fitted. Upon arrival in Southeast Asia, the package was hand-delivered to the printer, with a press run of 5,000 copies slated for delivery just prior to opening day.

Several weeks later, the public relations director received a letter from the division manager, enclosing a copy of the brochure.

"I hope you like it," he wrote. "The printer had a difficult time matching the exact shade of blue you specified, but you'll see that it was very close."

After an exchange of telexes, the public relations director's fears were confirmed. Despite the inclusion of color separations in the package, 5,000 blueline proofs had been printed and shipped to Canton.

Two Little Words

A seasoned New York publicist who represented many well-known personalities in the entertainment industry had a reputation for surmounting any difficulty.

He faced a major challenge on one occasion in the 1940's when an actress slated to appear in one of his client's productions arrived by ship in New York. With reporters and cameramen pressing him for interviews and photo opportunities, he was concerned about whether she could handle them. The difficulty was she spoke hardly a word of English.

Fortunately, the publicist had a chance to meet with her beforehand. He told her that no matter what questions she asked, she should answer every one of them with only two words, "men" or "money."

The resulting press coverage was ecstatic, portraying her as a vivid personality with an interest in only two things, both of which she'd be certain to find in abundance during her stay in America.

MANAGEMENT APPROVAL

The retired public affairs director for the port authority of a major East Coast city recalls a lesson he learned early in his career about securing approval from top management for a new publication.

While reviewing sketches with the artist for the first brochure he worked on, he spotted a glaring, obvious error.

"We have to change this," he said. "I can't take it upstairs until it's been corrected."

The artist laughed. "That's the 'third arm,'" he responded. "It's so obvious, they'll spot it immediately and believe they've made a valuable and constructive suggestion. Then, they'll feel they don't have to look at the rest of the layout as carefully and make other suggestions."

It worked out just as he'd predicted. The public affairs director and artist worked together harmoniously for many years, with every proposed layout containing an error as obvious as a "third arm" on a human figure.

Without fail, top management at the port authority, having spotted one glaring error, invariably expressed satisfaction with the rest of the layout and never questioned its basic concept.

HEADLINES, HEADLINES

Several years ago, the owner of a public relations counseling firm received an urgent summons to the office of the president of a West Coast entertainment company. The latter had terminated his contract with a large national agency with which he was dissatisfied and offered the account to the smaller firm.

In characteristic Hollywood style, his primary objective turned out to be personal publicity. He wasn't looking for much, he said, just his name in a headline once a week in the daily edition of *Variety*, the industry's leading trade publication.

The public relations counselor accepted the assignment and spent the best part of his weekend preparing an outline of his strategy and specific publicity objectives.

When he arrived in his office the following Monday, that day's edition of *Variety* was on his desk. There, across the top of a page, was a headline which contained the name of his new client.

The entertainment company's board of directors had fired the president over the weekend.

83-ALLE

RUNNING ON EMPTY

When public relations professionals get together, their favorite anecdotes invariably include ones about outrageous questions from inexperienced reporters.

The vice president of corporate communications for a major corporation has a particular favorite, posed by an enterprising young reporter after an aircraft accident.

Initial reports focused on a possible communications problem between the pilots and the control tower. Subsequent investigation revealed, however, the aircraft had been low on fuel, and after being instructed to make a go-around before attempting a landing, it had simply run out of fuel.

The reporter, assigned to write a follow-up story, decided to contact the company that manufactured the aircraft's jet engines. He obviously thought he had a new angle on the story.

After posing several general questions about the engines, he suspected he had the company on the defensive and determined to smoke out whatever they were trying to hide.

"Now, tell me," he demanded. "Just why did your engines fail when the aircraft ran out of fuel?

The company spokesman was completely at a loss for words. He couldn't think of a simple answer the reporter might understand and his silence was, of course, duly reported.

POLITICS AS USUAL

Despite the proverb "nothing succeeds like success," too much of it can backfire, as a leading public relations consultant discovered several years ago.

His firm was counsel to a midwestern state for its economic development and travel and tourism. It had conducted an aggressive, creative national campaign for several years with significant and measurable results.

During the campaign, new industry had been attracted to the state; 4,000 new hotel rooms were added and the hospitality industry had recorded an annual increase of $1.2 billion in revenues. The firm continued performing in an outstanding manner unaware of its political implications.

Opposition politicians were highly critical of the national recognition received by the governor, which they attributed to the public relations campaign. They claimed he was using the firm to advance his personal ambitions.

When the state legislature convened late in the year, economic development and travel and tourism were subject to heated debate. The result was that the entire budget was eliminated and the firm lost the account. Its chairman learned that successful public relations is sometimes not good politics.

ALLE

FRESH APPROACH

One editor who has worked on the staffs of several corporate publications took great pride in striving for freshness and originality in business writing.

For several years, he was given the task of preparing the chief executive officer's year-end message to employees.

Each year, he reviewed the messages which had been published for several years previously, then returned them to the files and labored over his typewriter to produce a fresh, original piece of prose.

Predictably, the chief executive officer's secretary would call a couple of days later to request copies of previous years' messages.

Just as predictably, his draft would be returned, accompanied by an approved text which was a virtual clone of several previous years' efforts, bereft of freshness or originality.

BEHIND THE LENSE

A highly regarded New York public relations advisor still mourned by numerous friends and admirers, had a favorite story involving his wartime service in the Pacific.

At the close of World War II, he'd been a combat photographer, and when the fighting ended, he accompanied U.S. forces to a number of islands which were never invaded, thence to Japan itself.

Many years later, having maintained his military connections, he happened to visit the headquarters of an Air Force general whose office walls boasted the usual array of awards, certificates, plaques and photographs.

One photo depicted the general descending from a transport plane. It showed, he explained, that he'd been the first American to set foot on that particular piece of Japanese soil.

"I'm afraid you weren't, sir," the public relations advisor replied. "I took that photograph and you'll notice that in order to shoot towards the aircraft, I had to precede you down the steps."

The general's face reddened visibly. He wasn't accustomed to being contradicted.

"Oh well," he finally retorted. "Photographers don't count!"

AVID READERS

Company publications enable management to communicate their concerns to employees — sometimes in unexpected ways.

A large manufacturing company published a slick monthly magazine which was distributed to hourly employees as they left the plant during each shift change. Stacks of the magazines were placed at each exit gate where the guards could pass them out as workers filed by.

One month, a pile at the main gate fell over. As the magazines slithered across the pavement, the guard closed the gate temporarily while he gathered them up and re-stacked them.

Meanwhile, a growing line of workers backed up inside the gate. Someone whispered, "It's a shakedown! Pass the word."

When the guard had picked up the magazines and re-stacked them, he opened the gate and the crowd filed through. Behind them on the ground where they'd been standing was a collection of micrometers, tape measures, calipers, pens, pencils and other small, easily concealed articles.

JON. L. ALLEN

NATIONAL COVERAGE

The president of a rapidly growing company decided to retain the services of a public relations firm for the first time. He was unfamiliar with publicity but extremely proud of his company's success in the marketplace with a line of useful but decidedly unglamorous products.

The account team at the public relations firm brainstormed ideas which could be developed into publicity. One of these was remarkably imaginative and was picked up by a major wire service for national distribution.

More than 200 clippings from daily newspapers throughout North America came back from a clipping service and were assembled into an impressive presentation.

The account supervisor and his assistant took the presentation with them to the next client meeting and spread them out proudly for the president's inspection. His eyes lit up as he pored over the clippings.

Then he bridled and became indignant. He pointed his finger accusingly at the table.

"What are you trying to pull here?" he demanded, "These are all the same story."

BIRD IN HAND

First prize in a contest sponsored by a sewing machine manufacturer was an all-expense paid three-day trip to New York City. The contest theme was "the most unusual item sewn on any make machine."

Hands-down winner was a spry, 70-ish lady who lived on a farm in Pennsylvania. She'd sewn red flannel underwear for her prize black Minorca hens to keep them warm during the molting season.

The public relations account executive who'd escorted her and one of her hens around New York was nonplussed when the winner impulsively handed her the bird in Pennsylvania Station. "Please keep her. You've given me an experience I'll never forget."

After a couple of days, her daughter and friends tired of attempting to catch a flying chicken in red underwear skittering around her apartment.

She was able to persuade a suburban editor to run a story. "Room and Board Wanted for Homeless Chick," the headline read, accompanied by a photograph of the black Minorca taken in the office of her husband, a dentist. Happily, a suburban home was found for the prize hen.

The account executive's husband was not so lucky. Two weeks later, a registered letter arrived summoning him before the ethics committee of the county dental society.

OPEN SKIES

A public relations counselor in the Southwest recalls his share of events at which something went awry, but he also tells fondly of one occasion at which the arrival of uninvited guests assured its success.

He was involved in an inaugural reception promoting a new air service at a small airport. Civic leaders, elected officials, people active in regional aviation and the local press were invited.

As the ceremonies started and the champagne uncorked, several helicopters approached the airport and landed a short distance away. Out stepped the state's entire Congressional delegation, accompanied by reporters from the major newspapers and local wire service bureaus.

Naturally, they immediately joined the party.

It turned out they were merely making a refueling stop on the way to another event elsewhere in the state. They had no idea they were about to become honored guests.

The public relations consultant received congratulations all-around. The civic leaders were thrilled and his client delighted with the news coverage of the inaugural. Although he'd been as surprised as anyone else at the time, he never went out of his way to deny he'd had a hand in the arrival of the helicopters.

83-ALLE

EMBASSY ROW

Public relations consultants often find no matter how good their proposals are, clients take their business elsewhere. And it's not uncommon never to learn the reason.

An experienced consultant in the nation's capital spent many months wooing a new account which he came close to losing for a reason his competitors have never experienced.

The year was 1963, with the New York World's Fair scheduled to open the following spring. A small nation in West Africa had contracted for a pavilion and needed public relations counsel. The consultant's proposal was accepted with enthusiasm by the nation's ambassador.

"It's a deal," the latter concluded. "I'll have the contract signed by our minister of economics next week while I'm home and bring it back with me at the end of the month."

After several weeks had passed without hearing from the ambassador, the consultant made some inquiries and learned there had been an upheaval in his nation's government. While on home leave, the ambassador had been arrested and shot. The consultant was distraught. Not only were months of effort wasted, but he'd rather liked the ambassador.

The quality of his proposal and the terms of the contract, however, saved the account. It turned out the minister had signed the contract and given it to the new ambassador to take to Washington.

INTRODUCTORY OFFER

The president of a public relations firm in California calls it "counter-marketing," but it's also a classic example of using effective copy to get results.

He recalls the story thus: Every year an elegant resort not far from a major racetrack was plagued with an invasion of prostitutes during the racing season. Day after day the ladies of the night placed their business cards on doors, pay phones, soft drink machines, bar stools, even in the men's restrooms. At first, management assigned the security staff to remove them, but the cards just kept reappearing.

Rather than advertise their actual services, the professional ladies took advantage of a nearby beach to promote themselves as "surfer girls."

Finally, the public relations manager for the resort came up with a more subtle solution to the invasion of the "surfer girls." For a few dollars several rubber stamps were ordered. Rather than remove the unwanted cards hotel security then left them where they found them after using the rubber stamps to add the words, "FIRST HOUR FREE."

FISH STORY

Several newsreel cameramen showed up many years ago at the invitation of a Florida public relations counselor to cover a fishing tournament. Most were union members, one was non-union, and the former decided the non-union cameraman should be excluded from the group. He was ordered back to shore.

After the first two hours, not a fish had been caught. The counselor's client was disconsolate. To avert a total disaster, he dispatched one of his staff to a fish market to buy some fish, take them to the tournament and tie them on the hooks so when contestants reeled in their lines, there would be fish to photograph. It seemed like a good idea; although, the public relations counselor wasn't too happy about the deception.

The non-union cameraman hadn't gone ashore as instructed. He shot film of the fish being tied to hooks, put in the water and reeled in.

While the other cameramen forwarded film to their editors, the non-union man had a better idea. He sold his film to a major network and scooped his competitors. His film revealed the deception and the fact none of the contestants had caught a single live fish.

FINAL JUDGMENT

A retired public relations consultant recalled an occasion when he was able to prove that publicity can be more cost-effective than advertising. A client had been directed by a Federal regulatory agency to advertise nationally that a small electrical appliance posed a hazard to users. The budget for a newspaper, radio and television campaign was estimated to be $8 million to $10 million.

In a court hearing, the consultant's client proposed a massive publicity campaign instead, starting with a press conference in Washington. The judge was willing to permit a one-week test period. The conference received national coverage and backup releases were sent to news media in local markets.

When the client returned to court a week later, his exhibits included a large map of the U.S., pin-pointing every known placement in the country, along with boxes of clippings and radio and TV tapes.

It was an expensive effort, involving a large number of people for a short period of time. However, the final bill was a fraction of the cost of an advertising campaign.

The judge agreed that the publicity was sufficient to meet the Federal agency's requirement and ruled against the need for advertising.

HOT SPOT

A California public relations consultant was formerly employed by a high technology firm which manufactured solar energy collection units. These were selected for a project co-sponsored by the government and a leading university.

Because numerous important guests were expected for the on-site dedications and start-up, she was asked to produce a suitable memento. Since the units were quite attractive, she located a supplier who could cast miniature versions in metal, then plate them and mount them on wooden bases.

However, when they were delivered, she learned that engineers have their own mindset. One colleague held one up to a window and told her with an expression of outrage, "the parabola doesn't focus on the central receiving tube."

Management seriously considered re-casting the mementos so they'd be technically perfect. But insufficient time remained before the dedication. Moreover, a new mold would have increased the cost substantially.

The engineer had a suggestion, as a result of which she spent the next several evenings in her office with a pair of tweezers pasting tiny pieces of mylar on the parabolas to make them reflect properly.

SPECIAL EDUCATION

More that 50 local schoolteachers thoroughly enjoyed a morning visit to a manufacturing plant on the occasion of the annual observance of Industry-Education Day.

A tour of the plant was followed by a steak luncheon and remarks by company officials. At its conclusion, each teacher was given a bagful of souvenirs. Included was a hardbound, illustrated history of the company from its founding to the present day.

At the undoubted prodding of their principals, each teacher sent a thank-you letter to the company's public relations manager. Most were sincere, if not particularly memorable.

One letter, however, has provided the public relations manager with a favorite anecdote he relishes telling to fellow professionals.

After several sentences thanking the company for its hospitality, one candid teacher wrote, "I want to thank you especially for the book about your company's history. I've been reading a chapter from it to my pupils each day and they enjoy it very much, since they are retarded."

WHITE WATER

A group of British journalists was making an escorted tour of scenic attractions in a mountainous state accompanied by the director of information for the state's department of tourist development.

One of the highlights of the tour was a white water rafting trip down one of the premier rivers in the state.

The day before the scheduled trip, the tour operator who would serve as their guide reported the river was too high and dangerous for rafting.

"What are we going to do then?" one of the journalists asked.

"Oh, we'll make the trip," he replied. "After I've arranged to lower the river."

The trip was made as scheduled and was a big success. Several of the journalists mentioned his feat with awe in their travel articles.

What he didn't tell them was a senior executive of one of the nation's largest hydroelectric power authorities planned to accompany them on one of the rafts and had already telephoned instructions upstream that the river be lowered to perfect rafting level for the day.

WEDDING BELLS

A traditional extra chore for many public relations practitioners has always been getting a wedding story about the boss's daughter into the society section of the Sunday newspaper.

One press relations manager at a Connecticut-based corporation had a good track record with such stories at the *New York Times*. When he began his career on a small daily newspaper he'd produced literally hundreds of wedding and engagement stories. He not only wrote them well, he maintained a good relationship with society editors.

One Monday morning when he arrived at his office, he was summoned by a senior executive whose daughter had been married the previous Saturday.

"I see you got it in the *Times*," the executive said, but he didn't appear too pleased about the story.

As it turned out, the *Times* had added something to the story about which the press relations manager had been completely unaware.

The bride had been married and divorced previously. While the *Times* considered this relevant, her parents apparently would have preferred to forget about it.

LOCAL COLOR

How to plan a grand finale for the dedication of a new 4,400-acre waterfront recreation area was a challenge for the public affairs director of a California city more than 30 years ago.

His friends in the U.S. Navy were delighted to help. They arranged for a line of underwater explosives to stretch across the bay, alternating red, white and blue smoke charges which would send up a wide plume of water. It would be impressive. And a spectacular surprise.

The mayor was briefed on the plan. After the speeches, he'd press a plunger to set off the Navy's explosives.

Everything went exactly as planned. A wall of red, white and blue water rose in the air as thousands cheered.

Within moments, the water was covered with the white bellies of dead fish. City employees spent the next three days collecting them.

There were letters to editors, critical editorials, calls to members of the city council and to the mayor's office.

The public affairs director never asked the Navy for another favor. When he asked his counterpart at the Navy base if he'd known there would be such a massive fish kill, the latter said, "Of course. But you never asked about it so we assumed you knew."

JON. L. ALLEN

CHRISTMAS MAGIC

A public relations counselor in Maine numbers among his clients a hospital for which he produces a Christmas story every year. Members of the cast are volunteers and the audience is comprised of local children.

Each show features Mr. and Mrs. Santa Claus, elves and reindeer, and involves someone being helped by the hospital.

The first year, the plot called for bad weather to force Santa Claus to make an emergency landing. After impact, it was discovered Rudolph the Red Nosed Reindeer's nose could no longer light to lead Santa on his way.

An emergency room team, headed by "Doctor Bill," came to the rescue and asked the children to cheer loudly for Rudolph's recovery. Christmas was saved and everyone joined in song as Rudolph led Santa on his way to deliver gifts.

Two weeks later, the counselor recalls, a five year-old boy was rushed to the emergency room with a badly cut hand. He sat calmly throughout the admissions process, his mother more upset than he. A nurse asked if he wasn't worried.

"Of course not," the youngster answered. "This is the hospital where Doctor Bill fixed Rudolph's nose."

The Christmas story became an annual tradition and a permanent part of the hospital's public relations program.

ᴸLE

GLOBAL VIEW

As he was developing a corporate advertising campaign, a public relations executive was fascinated by the diverse make-up of his company's research staff. Its scientists and engineers, boasting impressive academic credentials, were émigrés from England, Hungary, China, India, Australia and other nations.

He and his colleagues created a layout which featured a large aerial photo of the company's sprawling research labs, accompanied by small portraits of a dozen staff members. The text proclaimed boldly the company was a place where "research has an international flavor."

The first executives to pass judgment in the lengthy approval process loved it. The ad positioned the company as a global player, able to attract the best minds regardless of international borders.

It needed the opinion of only one senior vice president to kill it. At the time, corporate communications reported to industrial relations which was headed by an executive who was essentially a labor negotiator.

"Too damn many foreigners," was his reaction. "Take 'em out and show folks from several states instead of all them foreign countries."

SCHOOL DAYS

After 20 years as a journalist and magazine editor, followed by a stint in corporate communications with a couple of large companies, an Ohio public relations executive thought he was pretty knowledgeable. He succumbed to the lure of the academic world and accepted an offer to join a university faculty as an associate professor.

His first few weeks on campus were a heady experience as he looked forward to sharing his expertise in news writing and editing, production and media relations with his students. He spent long hours designing a curriculum, reviewing texts and preparing lecture notes. By the start of the first semester he was very comfortable in his new role as an educator.

Toward the end of the third week of classes, one of his students raised her had.

"Professor, do you mind if I make a suggestion?"

"Of course not," he responded. "I'm always open to suggestions."

"Well," the student continued, "why don't you invite a working professional as a guest speaker so we can learn what it's like out there in the real world?"

DELAYED ACTION

The chief executive officer of a large textile company was under pressure 20 years ago to dismiss its president.

On a Tuesday afternoon, he summoned his director of corporate communications and told him the president had "resigned" at an unscheduled board meeting at his home. His instructions were there would be no announcement until Friday.

The corporate communications director protested that would violate Securities and Exchange Commission and New York Stock Exchange regulations. Legal counsel agreed, so the chairman angrily agreed to wait until the following day.

Late that evening a local newspaper and radio station called, making a statement necessary by midnight. Any action by the chairman's stockbroker had clearly been thwarted.

The corporate communications director, naturally, became the scapegoat. Three months later he was dismissed for not following instructions, even though doing so would have been illegal for everyone involved.

Much later, he learned what had happened. An outside director who was also an unhappy major stockholder had called the press about the "so-called" resignation in order to hold the chairman to his agreement to dismiss the president and prevent him from backing out of it.

JON. L. ALLEN

NO CONTEST

For a product promotion, a publicist arranged to stage a teenage dance contest in California, the winners receiving a trip to New York. A consultant who worked frequently with teenagers thought her kids would love the contest and promised a dozen couples at contest time.

Judges from a dance studio, executives from the client company, reporters and photographers were on hand early. However, not a single contestant made an appearance.

"Where are the contestants?" the publicist demanded.

"Well, you never know about kids," was the response.

"What do you mean, you don't know about kids," the publicist screamed. "You're supposed to be the expert on kids." Still, no contestants showed up. She, not the consultant, had to face an impatient crowd in the ballroom.

Suddenly, the publicist remembered that two days before, by chance, she'd met the director of a summer camp and still had his business card in her briefcase.

Luckily, he was in his office. She told him if he could deliver a dozen kids in thirty minutes, her client would make a generous contribution to the summer camp.

He came, bringing sixteen teenagers by bus. The contest began and everyone had a marvelous time. The winners were awarded a trip to New York, press coverage was excellent and her client delighted.

MORE JAWS

A Miami publicist was once retained by an eccentric Frenchman who claimed he could harness a shark, then ride and steer the shark through the water.

Newspaper, magazine and television reporters were invited to cover a demonstration in an enclosed lagoon.

As the Frenchman attempted to attach the harness, the small shark selected for the demonstration got loose and attached itself to the Frenchman's leg. Everyone photographed it but doubted the story would ever see print.

By the time the publicist had succeeded in loosening the shark's grip on his client's leg, he realized he was losing everyone's attention. He needed to come up with a better ending.

Suddenly, he had an inspiration.

He asked the Frenchman who hadn't suffered any serious injury from the unexpected nip if he'd be willing to bite the shark. The Frenchman did. Half a dozen photographers recorded it.

The story was carried by both major news services and network television picked up a local feed, headlining it as that week's customary bizarre story from Florida.

BACKGROUND ONLY

When a luncheon speaker still hadn't arrived long after dessert and coffee had been served, the master of ceremonies stalled with every joke he'd ever heard, desperately trying to keep an audience of several hundred in the room. His public relations consultant realized that newspaper reporters were enjoying the jokes, but a local television crew was desperate. All they needed, they assured him, was five minutes.

Finally, the speaker arrived. His flight had been delayed by weather and he'd been rushed into a waiting limousine at the airport.

The public relations consultant was told by his client that all interviews would have to wait. It was an important audience and the speech had to come first.

He told the frustrated newspapermen as much, but was unable to find the television crew.

He'd underestimated their ingenuity. Since the speaker had been held in place by his seat belt for several hours, they were waiting at his first stop—the men's room.

A brief on-camera interview was conducted without interruption and appeared on the local station's evening news. The public relations consultant wondered if anyone besides himself noticed that it was shot against a white porcelain background.

CRISIS MANAGEMENT

The public relations director of a leading forest products company believes strongly that his local managers' greatest strength should be grace under pressure.

He knew he had just such a manager on his staff one day when his phone rang. It was one of his best regional managers.

"Just wanted to let you know," the manager reported. "We had 20 environmental protesters outside the gate this morning, but the plant manager invited them in for a meeting and they were gone before the local newspaper could get a reporter or photographer out here.

"Fortunately, they'd no sooner left than we had an explosion in the pulp mill, but there were no injuries."

The public relations director could hear sirens on the phone and inquired if it was a response to the explosion.

"No," the regional manager answered. "Now we have a fire in the plywood plant. I have to get over there and check that out. It's been a helluva day."

ALPHABET SOUP

When a U.S. cabinet officer made a highly visible trip to Japan, he was accompanied by a large press contingent. It fell to his director of public affairs to keep them happy during a grueling itinerary.

There were few opportunities for print journalists to spend time with the official, but television crews were able to capture some shots as the party crisscrossed the country by bus and helicopter.

At the end of a tiring day, the contingent headed back by bus to Tokyo. The ABC-TV correspondent asked directions to his network's Tokyo bureau.

"No problem," the driver assured him. "We can drop you off. We pass right by the building."

The driver dropped off the correspondent before the entrance to a large building with a huge, illuminated "ABC" sign, then he returned his other passengers to their hotel.

Four hours later, the ABC-TV correspondent stormed into the temporary pressroom at the hotel. The "ABC" building had been the offices of a Japanese company. His news bureau was in a different part of the city. It had taken him two hours and a fortune in taxi fares to get there. He'd also missed the nightly satellite feed to New York.

MOONLIGHTING

The public relations director of one of the world's largest textile companies assigned a photographer to shoot photos of several experienced employees on the job. One of the best shots, depicting an employee operating gleaming textile machinery, was selected for the cover of the company's annual report.

Production of the report proceeded smoothly until two days remained before it was scheduled on press.

As the report's designer recalls, he received a frantic call from the public relations director early that morning.

"You won't believe this!" the latter said. "But you know the photo we selected, the one with the employee operating the equipment? He's just been arrested for selling marijuana."

For everyone involved, "normal business hours" were forgotten. The printer rescheduled the press run. A new photo of another employee was taken on the next shift. Color separations were made overnight at additional expense. And the public relations director swears he noticed a few more gray hairs in his mirror the following morning.

Everyone involved cooperated splendidly. Less than two days later, the annual report was on press close to the original schedule as planned months in advance.

FOOD FOR THOUGHT

At least two experienced publicists have learned to be wary of promotions involving food. One learned his lesson in Florida, the other in California.

The first staged a publicity stunt with pretty girls in bathing suits throwing tomatoes at one another in an effort to draw attention to the state's largest winter crop ever harvested. It received nationwide news coverage.

The second, while promoting a new breakfast cereal, arranged to have a large container in a shopping mall filled with the product so news photographers could capture a group of youngsters romping in it.

Both promotions backfired. Sponsors, local officials and the publicist all received dozens of critical letters. Everyone was damned for their roles in wasting food while so many homeless and hungry people went without it.

Even worse was to come for the publicist for the cereal company, however. His client decided to salvage what remained of his reputation by donating it to a local zoo.

The zoo promptly turned down the contribution after examining the product. Its sugar content was inappropriate and, likely, might be harmful to their animals.

83-ALLE

THE SEVENTH DAY

A West Coast public relations counselor learned under embarrassing circumstances that what some people consider fun is just another day's work for others.

He'd arranged for a client to make an important announcement during a lavish buffet luncheon on a lovely Sunday at the client's magnificent hilltop home. Tables were covered with gourmet foods and fine wines uncorked. The counselor confidently told his client to expect at least 50 guests.

All was ready at noon. Half an hour later no guests had arrived. One o'clock passed and it was apparent no one was going to show up. Finally, three minor journalists arrived and, ignoring the superb buffet, headed for the bar.

His embarrassment was justified. Obviously, no one wanted to give up time during a lovely weekend for what the client considered fun, but what journalists considered work.

The counselor arranged a press conference several days later at a large hotel. Everyone who was invited came, the announcement was made with excellent results and the counselor, back in his client's good graces again, continued to represent him for many years.

GUEST LECTURER

The new speech writer at a major petroleum company was having a difficult time with his first effort for the chairman of the board. Although the material covered was just what the chairman had in mind and was polished and flowed smoothly, he'd already prepared three drafts. In despair, he asked one of his colleagues for suggestions.

His co-worker reminded him the chairman had spent the early part of his career as a professor at one of the nation's leading business schools.

"Remember, he's accustomed to speaking in front of a blackboard," he explained. "All you need to do is reorganize the material and number the points he raises, the solutions he proposes and his conclusions. Go back to your outline and put numbers in front of everything."

It worked like a charm. The fourth draft was virtually the same as the third, except for being organized like a lecture.

NIGHT CALLER

Shortly after he relocated to New York City to join a major corporation, a former newsman found himself extremely busy as principal spokesman during the early days of a nationwide strike. In fact, the first evening, he arrived home well after a dinner party his recent bride had planned long in advance.

"I'm so embarrassed," she exclaimed when he walked in. "The *New York Times* called three times. I was just about to serve dinner, so I told him we already have home delivery and hung up on him twice."

"What happened the third time?" her husband asked.

"Well, first he asked for you. Then, he told me he was a reporter. He saved the fact he was with the *Times* for last and pleaded with me not to hang up on him again."

The spokesman returned the call and the reporter, who subsequently became a good friend, kidded his wife about "home delivery" for several years thereafter.

LACK OF EVIDENCE

When an assistant commissioner for public affairs in a major city learned an important magazine had assigned a freelance writer to profile his boss, he rearranged the following week's schedule, set up background meetings and assigned his assistant to help with additional research.

The freelance writer had already completed several weeks work on his own, so was a knowledgeable companion during the week he "shadowed" the commissioner day and night. Every question he posed was thoughtful.

Several weeks later, the free lance writer called the assistant commissioner. He was extremely apologetic.

"My editor covered all my expenses and paid me a generous 'kill fee,' but he won't publish my piece," he said.

"What happened?" the assistant commissioner asked.

"It's not what he expected. He wanted me to turn in an article which would make the commissioner appear incompetent and corrupt. I spent several weeks on the story and I couldn't find any evidence of that. He's a really dedicated professional and that's not the story the editor wants."

SPRING FEVER

A well-established industrial company maintained its headquarters in New York, but rotated its annual meetings around the country to a different city each spring. Coverage by local business editors and trade publications was generally good, but national publications and wire services seldom sent a reporter.

The year the company held its meeting in Boston, the Thursday afternoon event was preceded as usual by several luncheons for local customers, editors and financial analysts. As the company's press relations manager escorted his guests to a reserved section in the meeting room, he spotted a familiar figure strolling down the aisle.

An assistant financial editor from the *New York Times* had seemingly made a special trip from New York to cover the meeting. Months of hard work was being rewarded.

Alas, it turned out such was not the case. The man from the *Times* owned a summer home on the Massachusetts shore, spring was in the air and the weather forecast was excellent. He'd jumped at the chance to get out of town for a long weekend, especially at his employer's expense.

He did stop at the *Times'* Boston bureau, however, and file a substantial story — much more than the meeting would have rated if it had been held a few blocks away from the *Times'* building in New York.

SHOW BUSINESS

The chief executive officer of one of the nation's leading airlines didn't visit Los Angeles often, but when he did, he expected a lot of attention. Each visit put the company's local public relations manager under intense pressure since, even if the visit had no news value, he was always expected to produce results.

Exclusive interviews were arranged, at least one press conference was scheduled and the chairman's arrival and departure at the airline's terminal were covered by several reporters and photographers.

Only the public relations manager's colleagues at corporate headquarters knew their local man was acquainted with numerous unemployed and retired actors, cameramen and journalists, many of whom could be called upon for a favor.

There was always great excitement when the chairman was in town and, fortunately, he never stayed long enough to notice that, despite all the attention he received, little real news coverage actually appeared.

LLE

TEMPERATURE RISING

A particularly well-known stockholder who attended numerous annual meetings every year could always be counted upon for several questions at each.

One year at the annual meeting of a medical supply company, she rose to ask her third question of the day. She said she'd recently purchased two thermometers manufactured by the company — one oral, one rectal. Why was it, she demanded, the rectal one was accurate, but the oral one was not?

Nonplussed, the company's chief executive officer was momentarily at a loss until rescued by the vice president whose division manufactured the thermometers.

"I can understand why you get an accurate reading on the rectal thermometer," he replied. "However, for the oral thermometer to register properly, one must be able to keep one's mouth shut."

TIGHT SECURITY

When rumors of preliminary merger negotiations between two leading companies in the same industry leaked to the *Wall Street Journal*, the chief executive officer of one of the companies was furious.

Every member of his public relations department was instructed to sign a statement that he or she had not met nor spoken with the reporter covering that industry during the previous month.

Once this had been accomplished, the company's public relations director called a staff meeting in his office.

"The chairmen of both companies are satisfied the leak didn't come from here and we weren't aware of their meetings," he said. "But, now I'd like to know what kind of a press relations program we have if not one of you has had any contact with the *Wall Street Journal* for over a month?"

83-ALLE

HOME DELIVERY

The public relations director of a Texas-based company was at a loss to understand why his chairman of the board preferred one local newspaper over another one.

As a former reporter and editor, the public relations executive had a much higher regard for the other newspaper, which offered superior national and international coverage, more complete business news and a first-rate editorial page.

The answer, as it turned out, had nothing to do with editorial content.

The chairman of the board lived in a rural area, his home approached by a long gravel driveway from the closest farm road. The newspaper he preferred was delivered directly to his door, while the carrier for the better newspaper would only leave it at the end of the driveway.

JON. L. ALLEN

CHAIRMAN'S CHOICE

For his annual report photograph, the office of the company's chief executive officer had been turned into a temporary studio by a prominent portrait photographer. A series of business-like poses were shot of the chairman seated at his desk to assure a variety of choices.

When the proofs were ready, the company's public relations director studied them carefully frame by frame and marked several which showed the chairman to best advantage.

Later, the chairman hardly glanced at the proofs, but pointed immediately to his first choice. It was not one of the selections which had been marked.

The public relations director was familiar with the shelves behind the chairman's desk, filled with memorabilia, books and photos of the chairman with several world leaders. It was there the chairman pointed when he explained his choice. It was the only frame in which a photograph of his grandchildren was clearly visible.

AWARD WINNER

Although an industrial plant had been on-line for nine years, all employee communications had been handled at the firm's headquarters, some 700 miles away.

With the arrival of a resident public relations manager, startup of a local newsletter became possible.

The first issue was ready in less than a month, filled with the grist of industrial public relations: promotions, service awards, suggestion programs, marriages and births, sports and social events. As with many such publications, it was mailed to employees' homes, to reach their families, as well as dissuade them from reading it on company time.

The Monday after the first mailing, a worker came into the public relations manager's office waving a copy. "Are you the editor of this paper?" he shouted.

"Yes, why?"

"This paper really got me in hot water. See that story about the $2,500 suggestion award. I'm the winner."

"That should make you feel pretty good," the public relations manger countered.

"It did," the worker continued. "But I didn't tell my wife about it. I bought a boat with the money and she doesn't know about that either. When I got home Friday, she ran out to the car yelling 'Where's the money? Where's the money?' I thought she was going to kill me."

ROUTINE PROCEDURE

There had been several homicides within a few days in a sparsely populated region of a western state. A newspaper reporter from a town just across the state line telephoned the public information officer of the state's bureau of investigation after each for details.

After the fifth murder, a man from the reporter's own town was shot while visiting a small community across the state line. In what had become routine procedure, the reporter called to inquire about the latest case. The public information officer provided information about the victim, the circumstances and status of the investigation.

Later in the day, the reporter called again, this time his voice somewhat shaky. The headline above his story in that day's edition had proclaimed, "Local Man Murdered." He'd already received calls from members of the man's family and friends pointing out that he was so far very much alive.

The public information officer acknowledged this to be the case and apologized for not making it clear that it had been a shooting, but not a fatal shooting.

There was a long pause at the other end of the line. Then, in a voice tinged with plaintive desperation, the reporter inquired softly, "Any chance he might die?"

33-ALLE

SHOW TIME

It was a great occasion and called for something special. A trade association had just signed the 500th exhibitor for its annual show, a landmark event.

Management decided on a huge birthday cake with 500 candles, which would be lighted by the president and other senior executives. It would be photographed in advance of the show so trade publications could feature it in their special show issues.

A cake that size had to be carefully designed, so the association's public relations counsel retained an artist to prepare a layout indicating precise placement of the candles and particulars about the forthcoming show.

All the association's senior executives gathered in a spacious conference room for the lighting ceremony.

The huge cake was wheeled into the room on a special platform, then unveiled as photographers and their assistants positioned themselves for the ceremony.

Every candle was placed precisely as planned, and the name of the association and location and dates of the show were clearly visible.

In the center of the cake, however, exactly where the artist had put it for the bakery's guidance, in capital letters, were the words "LOGO HERE."

TRAINING PROGRAM

The marketing communications manager for a Texas company wore many hats. He handled advertising, promotion and press relations, as well as hosting out-of-town visitors. These ranged from owners of companies planning to buy his firm's machinery to technicians sent for training.

On one occasion, his company's export agent called from New York to advise him a technician would arrive the following day for training on equipment being purchased by a technical institute in South America. Although it was short notice, a translator was secured and a "hands-on" training program scheduled with the equipment.

When the translator picked up the technician at his hotel, the latter's wife was with him, which was unusual. Fortunately, the truth emerged on the way to the plant. The visitor was not a technician at all, but the chancellor of his country's central institute of technology, where the equipment would be installed.

The marketing communications manager tore up the training program, assigned a bilingual secretary to take the wife on a shopping tour and called his contacts at local universities. By the time the chancellor had toured the plant and enjoyed a leisurely lunch, a complete new program was arranged. Not much other work was accomplished that day!

RELIABLE SOURCES

A favorite story of many corporate public relations staffers 30 years ago was one they related to prove lack of cooperation with the press simply isn't beneficial. It's a lesson learned many times since.

A major consumer products company absolutely refused any cooperation with one of the leading business magazines, which planned to profile the company.

The magazine went ahead and did the story anyway. Reporters and researchers talked to suppliers, distributors, customers, competitors, former employees, financial analysts, government regulators, union officials and other sources. The company's management, meanwhile, refused to answer questions and declined all requests for interviews.

When the article appeared, not a single fact or comment from the company was included, yet it was remarkably detailed, highly accurate and not very flattering.

The company's management learned, to its chagrin, there's a wealth of data and opinion readily available which it cannot control outside the walls of its gleaming corporate headquarters. Journalists willing to spend time and effort to collect and analyze it have little difficulty doing so.

Fortunately for the company, management subsequently realized they had nobody to blame but themselves.

PUBLIC SERVICE

When he retired after a career that spanned more than 30 years in journalism and public relations, an executive concluded he had the time and financial independence to undertake some worthwhile public service.

He learned his church was part of a coalition of more than 40 congregations which operated a food bank, assisted the homeless and recycled waste. Moreover, the coalition had a public relations committee.

With his experience, he was confident his talents would be of value. When he attended his first committee meeting, only three other people were present, none of whom appeared to have ever been employed professionally in public relations, nor were ever likely to be.

He participated in the meeting and made several suggestions. But, it was soon apparent his definition of public relations differed from that of the others.

He was somewhat taken aback when the committee chairman, an overbearing woman, asked if he owned a pickup truck or a station wagon. Actually, he owned neither.

His suggestions were heard politely, but he was never again invited to attend a meeting of the committee. He was obviously an outsider who didn't belong on their "turf."

MOB SCENE

A corporate vice president of public affairs recalls vividly his first publicity assignment.

He was employed by a small agency that worked for anyone who came through the door, including two luminaries with questionable connections who were opening a new nightclub. The grand opening would serve as a charitable fund-raiser with a personal appearance by a film star. His flamboyant boss promised a crowd of "beautiful people."

Opening night, he arrived early. The film star arrived on time, as did a throng of thirsty journalists. Absent, however, was his boss and a crowd of "beautiful people."

The owners, decked out in gold chains, were restive. "Where's da people?" one of them rasped.

Confidently, he responded, "Oh, you know discos never hop until midnight." By that time, the film star had departed and the journalists were staggering around. "Where's da goddam people?" the client muttered again, looking at empty tables.

After midnight, his boss appeared in a swirl of mink and jewelry, with her lilting, high-pitched "halloo." He propelled her towards the clients and without awaiting an explanation decided to call it a night.

He was with the agency only a few more months and never found out what happened to "da people." The newsmen hadn't even noticed. Their reviews of the new disco were ecstatic.

POINT OF VIEW

In the early 1950's, one of Texas' legendary oilmen opened an elegant luxury hotel which attracted worldwide attention and drew dozens of celebrities to Houston from New York, Hollywood and the capitals of Europe.

However, he had a somewhat embarrassing problem. The highway from the airport to the hotel passed the operating headquarters of his oil and gas company where drilling rigs, machinery, pipe and other pieces of equipment were stored when not in use. Several of his out-of-own guests chided him about the terrible "eyesore" which bore his name.

Since his ego was involved and his reputation was at stake, he called in a firm of landscape architects and instructed them to come up with a solution.

When the firm made its presentation, complete with sketches, a scale model and a detailed plan, his public relations advisor was invited to attend the meeting. The landscaping budget which was proposed ran into tens of thousands of dollars.

Before giving his go-ahead, the oilman asked his public relations consultant if he had any comments.

"Only one," was the response. "Why don't we just take down the sign?"

Following a period of silence in the room, the oilman escorted the landscape architects to the door.

FRAME OF REFERENCE

Public relations professionals confess to difficulty in defining precisely what they do. Communicating it to others is even more of a problem.

This became quite apparent to a Texas public relations consultant when she made a proposal to a prospective client. As a reference, she gave the name of the chief financial officer of a small publicly held company for which she'd worked harmoniously for some time.

The prospect called her reference.

The chief financial officer conceded she wrote and produced the company's annual report and interim shareholder reports. She also wrote all the company's news releases and arranged all the company's contacts with the business and trade press.

He also admitted she played an important role in planning and conducting the company's annual meeting, and she assisted the firm's marketing department in creating and producing most of its sales literature. Everyone at the company was very pleased with her work.

However, in response to the caller's question, the chief financial officer was very candid.

"No," he concluded. "I don't think she handles our public relations!"

LEFT SPEECHLESS

The vice president of public relations for a health services organization served as a guest speaker many times during his career.

On one occasion, he recalls, he was scheduled to deliver the final address to several hundred high school students at a statewide career day. Following the luncheon, the presiding officer rose to make some administrative announcements prior to introducing him.

"The buses which will take you on the city tour are parked at the west entrance to the hotel . . ." the teenagers didn't wait to hear the rest of her announcements. They rose *en masse* and rushed for the exits. She waved her hands frantically and seized the microphone. "Don't leave!" she pleaded. "We haven't heard our final speaker."

It was too late. The only people left in the hall were the speaker and a handful of apologetic officials.

The following year, the career day was held in another city and he again received an invitation to address the participants. Since he had an unused speech, he accepted, with the understanding there would be no announcements and no introduction. He would simply start speaking. Moreover, he stipulated the doors be closed and monitors posted at every exit to contain the teenagers.

He didn't lose a single member of the audience.

83-ALLE

WILD KINGDOM

The publicist for an annual sportsman's show in the Pacific Northwest knew that a clever photograph was always sure to capture the attention of newspaper editors.

Since the show featured a variety of wild and tame animals, he came up with what seemed a unique idea. He borrowed a live red fox. When it had been tranquilized and its legs tied together, he draped the animal across the shoulders of the young lady selected to preside as queen of the event. *Voila!* A living fox stole, complementing her gorgeous gown.

The girl's smile quickly turned into a look of bewilderment, then astonishment, and finally terror. She begged him to remove the fox, which apparently hadn't been completely tranquilized.

Naturally, he volunteered to take her gown to be dry cleaned. When he picked it up two days later, the cleaner said, "We sure had a job getting that stain out over the shoulders. What was it, anyway?"

The publicist replied, "If I told you, you wouldn't believe it."

JON. L. ALLEN

HOLLYWOOD BOULEVARD

Celebrity endorsements have been a marketing mainstay for decades, if not centuries, and public relations professionals sometimes become involved.

A big three auto maker once customized a sports roadster, painted it a special color and shipped it by truck rather than rail to California for presentation to a glamorous starlet.

For the auto maker's divisional public relations manager, the project was an enormous headache. At least, he consoled himself, the publicity would be worth the trouble.

Weeks went by without a report on the presentation. No photographs of the starlet with the car were received.

Finally, the company's Los Angeles zone manager confessed she'd never appeared for the presentation. Her agent had shown up and taken possession of the roadster, explaining that she'd given it to him to help satisfy some debt he'd paid off for her.

Later, it developed that all contacts regarding the celebrity endorsement had been exclusively with the agent and she'd been unaware of the arrangements. The auto maker's public relations manager concluded that, while the company had acted in good faith, they'd been swindled out of a very expensive car.

LEARNING CURVE

When an investor relations firm was selected by an independent petroleum company in Colorado, the client insisted the only way an account executive could learn the business would be to work on an oil rig for several days.

Although the latter pleaded lack of work clothes, the company provided him with everything, including work gloves and boots. It soon became apparent the roughnecks with whom he worked resented having to teach him the ropes. They seemed intent on giving him a hard time.

However, they watched in awe as the "greenhorn" lifted heavy lengths of pipe properly, shifting the weight until it was balanced. He seemed to know what he was doing.

Later, after a brief demonstration, the crew waited for him to connect a line improperly and be embarrassed with a dousing. However, it was they who were rewarded with a shower of crude oil instead of water. Every trick failed. The only mishaps on the rig happened to the roughnecks. Nothing happened to the account executive.

When the chief executive officer returned to pick him up, he was puzzled and remarked that for a "greenhorn" the account executive had done a remarkable job.

The latter explained he'd thoroughly enjoyed the change of pace. The experience brought back memories of the many summers he'd worked at his dad's oil refinery.

FELLOW VETERANS

An airline public relations executive who entered the academic world after he retired recalls receiving a resumé from a job applicant many years earlier which was one of the most impressive he'd ever read.

The applicant's credentials and professional experience as a journalist and in several corporate posts were ideal for a spot the executive needed to fill in Chicago.

However, the credibility of the applicant's resume was completely undermined by the section which listed military service. He indicated he'd held a responsible public information assignment from 1943 to 1946 in a particular office at Army headquarters.

By sheer coincidence, the executive who'd been so impressed with the resume had spent most of World War II in charge of that very office.

He responded to the applicant, requesting additional information about his wartime service and, needless to say, never heard from him again.

COMMAND
PERFORMANCE

In the months prior to World War II, a very senior civilian and military public affairs executive who was a reserve officer remembers his recall to active duty as a newly-promoted captain. Although he later became a paratrooper, he entered the Army in 1940 as an infantry officer.

His first day on post, he met with his new battalion commander, a somber, unsmiling lieutenant colonel with all the charisma of a sack of cement.

"What did you do in civilian life?" the colonel asked.

"I was a newspaperman . . . and I did a radio show."

"What did you specialize in?" the colonel inquired.

When he explained he'd been a motion picture editor, his new commander's interest was apparent. "What did you do on a job like that?" he asked.

"I saw every film that came to town."

"Every film?" he asked in awe. "You must have seen a lot of those B pictures!"

"That I did, sir."

"Well," the colonel grinned with the air of someone who'd just been struck by a great idea. "I've got just the spot for you. I'm giving you command of B Company."

RUSSIAN ROULETTE

The first American company to print its annual report in Russian found its biggest obstacle to be delivering them to readers at the height of the Cold War. The company's public relations director had a solution. He mailed a few at a time in plain envelopes, franked with attractive postage. A great many reached the intended recipients.

His company's accountants, however, criticized his strategy. The reports were printed in Europe, so they reasoned it would be cheaper to affix labels there and ship them in bulk by surface mail. The following year, several thousand Russian-language annual reports were shipped accordingly, inspected at the Soviet border and destroyed.

During the following four years, the public relations director's strategy was used and the company gradually became well-known in the Soviet scientific community.

When the company's chief executive officer was invited to the Soviet Union as a guest of the prestigious Academy of Sciences, he was the first American industrialist so honored. Within a year, a trade agreement was signed.

The company's public relations director recounts with satisfaction that, when his chief executive officer went to Moscow, not a single accountant or lawyer accompanied him, but his public relations director was a key member of his company's negotiating team.

SOUND BITE

When foreign espionage was in the news, the director of communications for a large research institute with several government contracts was invited to appear on local television to explain his employer's security precautions.

The television anchorwoman conducted an on-camera interview with one of the institute's labs in the background. Her first question revealed she intended to conduct the interview according to her own story line: "How many of your secret projects have been leaked to the Soviets?"

The director of communications explained patiently that classified information was strictly protected. Security procedures were required by Federal law and the institute's own regulations. No one without an appropriate clearance and a "need to know" even had access to classified data.

The anchorwoman's subsequent questions, rather than being responsive to his answers, proved increasingly that he was being used as a foil. He emphasized repeatedly that the institute's security precautions were extremely effective.

His on-camera interview was aired on the evening news, edited for brevity. At its conclusion, the anchorwoman, accustomed to always having the final word, told viewers in a tight close-up, "but he didn't say it *couldn't* happen."

DUE CREDIT

In order to enhance the quality of his department's news and feature writing, the vice president of a major corporation hired a new director of editorial services. Although he'd written numerous magazine articles and several successful non-fiction books, the new man had never previously been employed by a corporation.

His first assignment was to research and write the lead story for a press kit about a major engineering and construction project in the Middle East. His text was marvelously detailed, superbly phrased and captured the admiration of everyone in the department.

When the vice president read it, however, he had one reservation.

"It's a wonderful article, well-researched, highly readable and informative, but there's something missing."

"Oh, I gave it my really best effort," the writer responded. "What did I leave out?"

"The name of our company," the vice president smiled.

ADVANCED DEGREES

A Texas public relations consultant recalls the only time he was stymied during a new business presentation.

He'd been invited to propose a marketing communications campaign for a local radio station and asked for ten days to complete the necessary research, evaluate listeners' perceptions and prepare a proposal. Then, he met with the station's board of directors.

"The station is highly respected in the community," he reported. "You're doing many fine things. Most of your listeners have high praise for you.

"The only negative I've been able to find are those atrocious billboards around town. The art is awful and the message is absolute nonsense."

The station's chairman of the board bristled. "How many degrees in art do you have to support your conclusion?"

"None," he answered. "I just know my business. I know the public. And, I know what works in your business."

"Well!" said the chairman. "My wife has several advanced degrees in art, and she designed those billboards."

The consultant realized his research had been a waste of time and he was unlikely to be awarded the account. He rose to leave. There wasn't much left to say.

"I still think the billboards are sheer crap," he retorted as he walked out the door.

BIRTH PAINS

When a national news service expressed interest in doing an article about a large medical center in a western state, the center's assistant director of public relations considered several personality possibilities. Among her ideas was a story about a young woman who'd just given birth to quintuplets.

An interview was arranged but she soon sensed reluctance by the young mother to meet with a reporter. As it turned out, her reluctance had nothing to do with the birth and subsequent loss of two of the quintuplets.

"Look," the assistant public relations director said. "We can call this off if you don't want to do it."

A week later, she learned the real reason the young mother wanted to avoid any recognition in the media. It was not to protect the privacy of her three surviving babies.

She and the father of the quintuplets were runaways and her parents had obtained fugitive warrants to find them and return them to their hometown in the Middle West.

Her story might have been a good news feature, but the medical center's assistant director of public relations decided that particular young woman already had more than enough complications in her life.

UNSPOILED VIEW

The public relations director of a university had the task of coordinating beautification of a campus expansion, serving as liaison between a landscape architect and a garden club which had volunteered to accomplish the work.

In the former's absence, club members planted trees and shrubs, some of which were not on the plan. A sturdy young oak tree was planted in front of a picture window. In a few years it would hide the building, which would not please the donor whose name was on the building. The public relations director called the landscape architect.

"Not to worry," the latter said. "I'm meeting with them on Saturday. Some 'public relations' is called for." As he toured the campus, he beamed his approval. "This is lovely," he told the ladies. "Your selections are perfect."

When he spotted the little oak tree he examined it carefully, touching each leaf with his fingertips.

"Such a delight!" he exulted. Then, a frown crossed his face. His gaze roamed from the tree to the horizon. With sorrow in his voice, he turned to his audience.

"Ladies, this little tree is not happy here. I hope it can survive." The next day, the ladies transplanted the little tree to a new location. The crisis was resolved. The ladies were happy. The president of the university was happy. And, the little tree was happy.

HOME RUN

The chairman of a large public relations firm has ceased being surprised by capricious requests from important clients. He wasn't quite prepared, however, for a request from one of his most important clients, posed at the end of an account review. The client asked if he could arrange a meeting with the owner of a major league baseball team.

"Why do you want to meet him?" he asked.

"Because I want to buy the club," his client answered candidly. So have dozens of others, hit by one foul ball too many, thought the chairman. Anxious to get off the hook, he called the club's president the following day and learned the owner was in Florida.

"The team's not for sale," he was told, as if he hadn't been aware of that for several years.

However, a dinner meeting was arranged with the understanding it would only be an opportunity to get acquainted. His client and the owner, surprisingly, spent several hours together, charmed each other and agreed they might do business together "some day."

That day arrived a few months later when the public relations counselor was asked to prepare a news release announcing the team's new ownership. One reason he's especially relished the experience is that, in its first season under new ownership, the team won the World Series.

DRAWING CARD

During difficult economic times some years ago, the longtime investor relations manager at one company was admonished to reduce expenses for the annual meeting.

Rather than hold the function at a hotel or in a rented hall, his financial vice president instructed him to hold it on company premises. The only satisfactory space was an auditorium in the company's sacrosanct, highly secure research center to which access was normally restricted. That was where he was told it would be held.

None of the company's executives realized beforehand how much allure the location would have for stockholders, many of them employees, retirees, suppliers and competitors. That year's attendance broke all previous records and the arrangements proved completely inadequate. The meeting was chaotic.

It also proved to be a setback in the investor relations manager's promising career with the company. The firm's senior executives made him the scapegoat for the debacle and transferred him to another position. He was never again given the responsibility for arranging an annual meeting.

JON. L. ALLEN

POLITICAL ADVANTAGE

Three executive vice presidents were candidates for the post of chief executive officer of a worldwide consumer products company. The firm's board of directors selected the one with a strong marketing background.

The executive vice president for finance thereupon instructed the public relations director that all speeches and statements by the new chairman would be routed through him for review and approval. The process began with the first speech to be delivered to an outside audience. A highly talented speech writer recalls preparing a dozen drafts, each of which was routed as instructed and rejected without explanation.

Finally, the executive vice president for finance gave up on the process and told the speech writer to work directly with the new chairman. The next draft was approved without change.

The speech writer realized the rejections had nothing to do with the quality of his work. The chairman was usually pleased with it. He'd been rejecting speech drafts as a political device to establish distance between himself and the executive vice president for finance with whom he'd been until recently co-equal.

CAMPAIGN TRAIL

Long before the term "public relations" was coined, a prominent newspaperman was known to freelance as a publicist while continuing to hold down his regular duties. He always enjoyed relating the circumstances involved in his first notable success in the "new" profession of public relations.

Much to his surprise, he received a phone call one day inviting him to a luncheon with three strangers. After they introduced themselves, they got directly to the matter on their minds.

They wanted him to launch and manage a campaign for the nomination for governor of the president of a major university so they could rid themselves of him. They were unhappy with his administration of their alma mater and felt he'd only leave the university if offered the possibility of government service. The fee mentioned was hard to resist, so the journalist accepted the assignment.

The candidate duly vacated his chair as president of the university, received the nomination and was elected governor of the state.

In later years, he attained national prominence and continued in public life, but the university's trustees had long since selected a president more to their liking.

CANDID CAMERA

When automotive safety became a subject of national debate in the late 1960's, a television network dispatched a crew to Detroit to capture industry comments. It would be included in an in-depth special scheduled for prime time.

The public relations staff at a major auto maker arranged meetings with top executives, the final session being an extensive on-camera interview with the company's director of automotive safety, a scholarly and articulate scientist respected throughout the industry.

The company's public relations staffers, most of them former newsmen, were surprised the interviewer's questions ranged from the trivial to the provocative and seemed unnecessarily repetitive. However, the company scientist acquitted himself superbly.

After the network crew had left for the airport, one of the public relations staff went to tidy the interview room before leaving for the day. In it he found a file folder containing the complete script for the news special, obviously written weeks before going to Detroit. The crew's visit to the company had apparently been a sham, merely a device to record on-camera quotes which could be spliced into the program out-of-context.

That's the way the news special aired on the network.

83-ALLE

GREEN REVOLUTION

When a large company in the Middle West was caught in a cost squeeze, its corporate communications department developed a successful cost-awareness campaign in which every department was urged to produce a ten-percent savings.

Concurrently, without the department's prior knowledge, as part of redecorating the corporate headquarters, green plants were installed in hallways, lobbies, offices and reception areas. Employees were in an uproar. They were even more incensed when they learned maintenance costs for the greenery amounted to several thousand dollars every month.

The company's management responded to the clamor by ordering the plants removed. As florists carried the plants from the building, several secretaries asked if they might keep some for personal use.

"Sure," one of the florists responded. "Once they've been in a commercial building, we're required by state law to throw them in a landfill dump." Another uproar ensued. The incident became an example of waste which was long-remembered.

In assessing the incident, the corporate communications department concluded cost-awareness and redecorating at the same time had sent employees conflicting messages. Management had not thought far enough ahead to anticipate the reaction and, worse, hadn't sought any advice either.

PLAIN FOLKS

The senior public relations executive for a diversified conglomerate often accompanied his chief executive officer on trips to various parts of the country. One of his chores was to arrange meetings with business editors or newspapers in cities in which the company had operations.

Because the firm's corporate culture was low-key and unstructured, the chief executive officer seldom let his intellectual qualities show. He tended to be informal and folksy, sort of shuffling his toe in an imaginary sand pile and peppering his remarks with plenty of "shucks" and "by gosh," while spinning a yarn to make a point.

It worked well. Most editors with whom he met profiled him favorably. He soon developed a reputation as an unusually easygoing business leader.

However, as the public relations officer recollects all too vividly, his boss' style failed to work in one of the major cities in the Deep South.

After a few minutes of conversation, the business editor of the local daily newspaper interrupted him.

"I like your style, but I also did my homework," he explained. "After The Hotchkiss School, Harvard College, Yale Law School and a stint in the State Department, a good 'ole 'country boy' you're not."

THE BLUES

The deadline for a real estate investment firm to publish its first annual report was near. The text was in type, and the designer's work was well-received in the executive suite. All that remained was a decision about the cover.

Since photographs had been used inside, it made sense that the cover should be restrained. The company's board of directors met and decided it should be blue.

Several meetings were held at which the designer presented samples — light blue, dark blue, gloss blue, matte blue. Each time the chairman of the board shook his head.

"No," he said. "These aren't right." The designer sensed he'd already seen the exact blue he wanted.

"Perhaps you can show us a sample and we'll match it," she suggested.

At the next meeting, the chairman dropped a four-inch piece of steel on the table, referring to it as his "color chip." It was a distinctive iridescent blue and he'd removed it with difficulty from his imported European sedan the previous evening.

The color was easy to match and the slight additional cost well worth it. When the annual report was delivered, the chairman was delighted, but never did explain how he'd managed to pry his "color chip" loose.

JON. L. ALLEN

FINAL DRAFT

A talented young public relations professional who later rose to a top post in a counseling firm was handed a tough assignment after a few weeks on his first job. He was assigned the task of writing a speech for the chairman of a client company who, despite the fact he'd never finished high school, had become a successful business leader.

The young man tackled the task eagerly. His previous writing assignments had been well-received. After a week, however, he was crestfallen. His first five drafts were written, revised . . . and rejected. All the client could offer was: "It's not what I want."

Finally, on the morning of the day the speech was to be delivered, a final draft was grudgingly accepted.

Some years later, after several promotions, the young professional had risen to a senior post in his firm, which had never lost that particular client's account. One day, he had to discuss a current campaign with the assistant to the chairman of the company.

"You know," the latter said, "the chairman speaks fondly of you often and is sorry you don't write his speeches any more. He says nobody has ever been able to write anything really good for him recently. You're the only one who could tell instinctively what was on his mind and put into words exactly what he wanted to say."

83-ALLE

LIGHTS OUT

When New York City experienced a blackout during a widespread power failure some years ago, media throughout the country naturally asked local power companies if a similar disaster might be possible in their cities.

In a videotaped interview, the chief engineer of a power company in Texas assured viewers such could never happen in his city. He praised the company's computer monitoring system, back-up generating capacity and controls. At the time, his colleagues in the public relations department thought he'd been supremely overconfident.

Their fears were confirmed a few weeks later, when the "impossible" happened on a Sunday evening in October. Much of the city was plunged into darkness by a system-wide outage and, even though power was restored within four hours, the incident received extensive news coverage.

The utility's assistant manager of public relations fielded dozens of calls and set up an impromptu press conference. The incident confirmed one of his most basic professional principles: never say "never."

What really grated, however, was that his boss was on two weeks vacation in Virginia and had no idea what had happened until he read about it in the following day's newspaper.

LOST IN TRANSLATION

Some years ago, the corporate secretary and the public relations director of an oil company planned to publish the annual report in three languages. Their plan was "top secret," both inside the company and to all outsiders.

Somehow, the local bureau manager of the *Wall Street Journal* learned of their plans and reported it. When it appeared, the corporate secretary was furious.

"We're the laughing stock of the industry," he fumed. "All the majors will do the same thing . . . faster, better and bigger. We have to cancel our plans." His ego had been badly bruised.

Several months later, when major oil company annual reports appeared, not one of them had a foreign language version. The public relations director called his counterparts at six major competitors to inquire if it had been considered that year.

All had the same response: "When we read about your plans in the *Wall Street Journal*, we decided not to go ahead this year as a professional courtesy." The corporate secretary was still furious.

"I'll bet you put them up to this just to make me look silly," he sputtered.

The public relations director didn't feel his corporate secretary needed any help with that.

ANGELS OF MERCY

Veterans of World War II who began their careers in public relations as junior officers assigned to coddle newsmen recall some unusual experiences.

One former public affairs officer remembers the time he was sent to Charleston to escort reporters and cameramen to the arrival of a hospital ship. Wounded troops would disembark, then be flown to hospitals throughout the country close to their hometowns. Victory in Europe was at hand, and humanitarian stories were good copy.

For two days, heavy fog delayed the vessel's arrival. Reporters and cameramen blamed the weather on the public affairs officers. A few poker games helped pass the time.

Finally, the ship docked; a band played popular music; beribboned officers and local politicians were lined up to welcome the wounded fighting men.

After the gangplank had been lowered, the first passengers began to disembark . . . a long line of khaki-clad Army nurses. Every single one was pregnant.

The newsreel cameramen were ecstatic. Colonels and majors went berserk, shouting, "seize those cameras, detain the reporters." Unfortunately, they found themselves giving orders to each other. Not a single junior officer had stayed around long enough to savor their wrath.

JON. L. ALLEN

CHRISTMAS SPIRIT

A public relations writer at a large Chicago bank prepared quarterly news releases summarizing the bank's views on the economic outlook and consumer attitudes. One year, during a recession, the consumer survey revealed that financial strains would affect Christmas gift-buying.

When a *Wall Street Journal* reporter called to probe beyond the statistics, he explained the numbers indicated consumers were substituting basic necessities for luxury items, terming it a "socks and underwear" Christmas.

As the youngest of several children of a wire service editor, he recalled his own family's Christmases. To add a few more boxes under the tree, his mother filled several with socks and underwear purchased on sale for each of the children.

Several days later, he received a summons to the office of one of the bank's senior vice presidents.

"What's this nonsense about socks and underwear?" he demanded. "Have you forgotten you work for an important bank?"

"The way I see it," he replied, "it was an opportunity to reveal the human side of banking which is rarely displayed in the numbers. And, to be quoted, one must say something quotable."

3-ALLE

DRY SPELL

Publicizing a particular brand of bottled water isn't easy as the staff at a public relations firm found out. At least, that is, until a major league baseball team moved to town.

A magnificent new stadium had been built and officially opened with great fanfare. There were an ample number of concessions selling refreshments on every level. Then the fans, and the local press, discovered that "accidentally" there wasn't a single drinking fountain in the stadium!

Not only did the press jump on the story, but seeing a great opportunity, so did the public relations firm. It recruited the account executive's young son with his little toy wagon, stocked it with several gallons of bottled water and stationed the youngster outside the stadium entrance. There he struck a vendor's pose, holding up a handwritten sign for all to see with the words "LAST CHANCE FOR WATER."

It resulted in widespread publicity for the client, including a front-page photo in the city's leading newspaper. And . . . the addition of water fountains to the stadium.

ROAR OF THE CROWD

Details can make a difference. And they are invaluable for smart planning, as one West Coast public relations consultant can attest.

One of his clients had sponsored a float in one of the nation's most colorful annual parades and been fortunate to secure the reigning Miss America to grace it. Another particularly elaborate float carried the three lovely daughters of the state's governor.

The public relations consultant for the first float knew, however, that all photographers would be positioned on a platform on one block on the right side of the street.

He told Miss America to keep her eyes to the right all the way down the block. "Just ignore the thousands of spectators cheering in the stands on the other side."

As it turned out, the governor's daughters hadn't been given the same advice, so when they heard loud cheering on the left side of the street, they quite naturally turned and waved in that direction.

The result: most photographs of the parade which appeared in national magazines featured Miss America's float with the sponsor's name clearly visible on the side. No photographs of the governor's daughters could be found in local or national publications.

CAMPAIGN TRAIL

During a gubernatorial campaign in a small eastern state, one candidate's campaign workers always returned from lunch with results of an informal poll, the result of asking cab drivers, waitresses, sales clerks and others for whom they planned to vote.

The public relations counselor who handled press relations for the candidate disdained to participate.

One day, however, he had a change of heart. After visiting the newsroom of the state's largest newspaper, he found himself alone in an elevator with one other man. He asked him for whom he was going to vote.

In response, the man named an obscure candidate for a tiny political party. Amazed, the counselor asked shy.

"I always vote for myself," he responded. "I'm the candidate. Here's my card."

Back at campaign headquarters, the counselor told his colleagues they might as well shut down. The race for governor was a lost cause. His informal lunch hour poll had found that 100 percent of those surveyed planned to vote for the obscure candidate.

Informal polling fell into disfavor. However, the counselor's candidate did win the election and served two terms in the governor's mansion.

CLEAN SLATE

The corporate communications director of a *Fortune* 500 company received an irate call from his chief executive officer one morning and hastened up to the latter's office.

The chairman held a copy of his company's latest annual report in his hand. Inside its gorgeous cover, every single page was completely blank. Attached to the report was a sarcastic letter from an institutional portfolio manager on Wall Street, indicating he'd found the report "of no particular interest."

Nonplussed, the corporate communications director promised an answer immediately, his heart racing as the elevator all-too-slowly took him back to his office.

He called the design firm, which called the printer, which, in turn, called the mailing house. He was soon able to breathe a sign of relief.

The printer had sent the mailing house one dummy, hand bound copy—one only—to enable them to verify proper fit in the envelope, adjust their machinery accordingly, weigh the report and set the postage meter for the correct amount. Thousands of other copies had been mailed without a problem.

3-ALLE

WHERE'S THE BEEF

A Texas public relations consultant with a wicked sense of humor recalls the times he arranged sportsmen's shows in Los Angeles to encourage fishermen, hunters and campers to visit the High Sierras.

Like his colleagues, he dressed in western garb with jeans, boots, bandana and a ten-gallon hat.

One show was held in an auditorium in a predominately Jewish neighborhood. After the first couple of days, he tired of the bland food available in the auditorium and ventured across the street to a small delicatessen for a pastrami sandwich.

When he sat down at the counter, an elderly waitress took his order. After glancing at his outfit, she inquired, "Are you Jewish?" He replied he was indeed.

"I never saw a Jewish cowboy before," she declared, shaking her head in disbelief. His response slipped out without a moment's hesitation, consistent with his years of experience at fielding unusual questions.

"Who do you think rides herd on the kosher beef?"

"Of course!" she exclaimed, muttering to herself as she walked to the kitchen.

It made perfect sense to her.

JON. L. ALLEN

SQUEEZE PLAY

An aggressive consumer affairs reporter at a Chicago television station relished accusing companies which she suspected of attempting to cheat consumers.

On one occasion she aired a report accusing a consumer products company of selling less than the claimed number of sheets on a roll of toilet paper.

The company flew a public relations staffer, a packaging engineer and an attorney to Chicago to rebut her claim. Company executives were baffled, because the sheets were counted by machine and trimmed in multiples of ten.

The three men took off their jackets, rolled up their sleeves and started counting sheets on three rolls of tissue purchased by the station. The count was accurate. The station sent out for six more rolls of toilet paper. Again, the count was accurate. In fact, it was higher than claimed, usually by as many as ten additional sheets.

It turned out the reporter's researcher hadn't counted the number of sheets. He'd simply measured the length of a roll and divided by the length of a single sheet.

As a postscript, the incident was the subject of a humorous column in the *Chicago Daily News*. The writer always enjoyed tweaking the consumer affairs reporter's ego with some choice barbs.

MEDIA RELATIONS

When asked to announce the expansion of a mine in a remote region, the press relations manager of a large mining company sought advice from one of his company's engineers who'd visited the facility frequently.

He inquired about local newspapers or possibly a radio station which might be interested in a story about how the expansion would affect employment and the local economy.

"There aren't any media there," the engineer told him. "But I can arrange for the minister to announce it in the local church on Sunday, then everyone within a hundred miles will know about it by dinnertime."

JUMP START

When a large manufacturer of sporting goods and apparel planned an open house at a new plant in the South, the services of a local public relations firm were retained.

The firm's account executive developed a program based on meetings with members of the plant's management. Since the facility was relatively new, the open house would serve as an introduction to the community. Good coverage in the local press was a high priority.

When the account executive interviewed the plant's personnel director, he learned the latter was also a Baptist minister. Moreover, his hobby was skydiving. The account executive recognized a natural opportunity.

On the day of the event, a crowd of more than 1,000 gathered on a broad lawn in front of the plant. Employees and their families and invited guests were all in place.

A small plane flew directly over the plant and the personnel director jumped. He guided his parachute towards an open space on the lawn, walked over to a microphone and delivered the invocation.

The account executive's judgment was right. Local press coverage was all he'd hoped for, with the minister's descent from the heavens prominently featured.

SECOND SEATING

A retired public relations executive who often arranged private dinners for his chief executive officer did a great deal of research prior to planning the seating arrangements. Often, when there were as many as 100 guests, the chief executive officer did not know them all personally.

After several meetings and phone calls, the public relations executive agonized over seating everyone to the best advantage for his chairman and the company. Several days in advance, he diagrammed table arrangements and arranged place cards in a folder.

He and his wife always arrived well before the first guests. They reviewed arrangements with the staff, then set the place cards according to his carefully-researched plan.

The chairman and his wife also arrived early in order to greet guests as they entered. Virtually every time, the public relations executive noticed that while he was briefing the chairman on the guests and the evening's program, the latter's wife busied herself moving from table to table and rearranging place cards.

He knew she was not acquainted with many of the guests, so he surmised that was simply her way of showing him that, despite all his careful planning, she made the final decisions at company-sponsored functions.

JON. L. ALLEN

MOTOR CITY

Business publications generally do an excellent job of checking facts, but they've been known to slip up on a detail or two. A corporate public relations executive recalls the time he pointed one out to the managing editor of a leading business magazine. The publication had done a profile on his company's chief executive officer in which one of the latter's typical days was described.

The article was generally favorable, depicting the chief executive officer as an astute business leader. However, one small detail caused consternation and embarrassment in the executive suite and consequently in the public relations department. The public relations director received his instructions and called the magazine.

"In addition to being our chief executive officer," he explained to the managing editor, "the chairman also sits on the board of directors of the Chrysler Corporation. He does not, absolutely does not arrive at his office in the morning or leave at the end of the day in a General Motors product."

Obviously, the reporter who'd written the story had never worked in the magazine's Detroit bureau and failed to realize such details can be taken very seriously.

SUMMER VACATON

A corporate public affairs executive who was also a reservist performed his annual duty in the Pentagon each summer. While called upon to handle delicate responses to the Congress and the White House, he also had a talent for spotting abuses.

One year, a fellow colonel asked him for advice regarding a call he'd received from an aide to a prominent senator. The caller had requested a country briefing for a distinguished educator about to leave on a trip to Europe.

By coincidence, the reservist and the senator's legislative assistant had gone to college together more than 20 years earlier and remained good friends.

A call to Capitol Hill confirmed his suspicion. The young aide had only been in the senator's office a few weeks and the briefing was for a personal friend. The "distinguished educator" was a schoolteacher planning a Mediterranean vacation. She was unknown either to the senator or senior members of his staff.

"Forget about it," the legislative assistant advised. "That's the last time she'll use the senator's name to ask for a personal favor. Moreover, it's also the last time she'll call the Defense Department from this office."

POODLE POWER

When two executives of a public relations firm met with the president of a pet food company many years ago, they were astonished to find him eating lunch from a can of dog food.

"It's excellent," he remarked about the food, which looked like meatballs. "And nourishing. I eat it regularly."

"Would you do this at a press conference?" they asked. Of course, he responded.

The press was intrigued and a large contingent turned up to watch the president and a poodle by the name of Snowflake share a luncheon plate. Unfortunately, the poodle refused to eat. The president finished the plate by himself, explaining the lights and attention had probably ruined her appetite. It turned out weeks later the dog's trainer had fed Snowflake prior to the press conference. The public relations executives could have killed him.

Summoned to the president's office the next day, they expected the worst. However, the president had received calls for competitors, customers and friends all over the country about his "coup." He was delighted.

The story eventually developed a life of its own. Years later, when a feature writer for the *Chicago Sun Times* died, his obituary included an anecdote about the story he'd written about the poodle who refused to eat dog food while the company president told the press it made an excellent lunch.

3-ALLE

GAME PLAN

Because the manager of an industrial plant in Ohio was involved in a local youth football league, his public relations manager had to handle the league's publicity.

The editor of the city's only daily newspaper was not a football fan and insisted there was no readership for coverage of the league. He refused to cover any games or even print results.

"Do you mind if I prove there's a demand?" the public relations manager asked him.

"If you can prove our readers are interested, we'll print the scores," the editor responded.

Prior to the next slate of eight games, the public relations manager instructed every coach to tell all the players, their siblings, parents, classmates, neighbors and friends to call the newspaper and ask for the final scores.

So many people telephoned the newspaper's sports editor they blocked other incoming calls for several hours.

The following week, the newspaper's sports section carried a brief summary of every game in the league and, to this day, continues to provide regular results for local youth football.

JON. L. ALLEN

BIRTH PAINS

A major airline had a run of unfavorable publicity some years ago until, one day, its public relations director learned a passenger was about to give birth in the air. "The flight attendants have her on a pile of blankets in the galley and are assisting in the delivery. The captain has asked for immediate clearance into Atlanta," his assistant reported.

The pubic relations director had just taken a call from a wire service reporter on another subject and, seizing the opportunity, filled him in on the miracle of birth aloft.

"Names, Bill?" he asked. "Flight number? Time of arrival at Atlanta? Who's the captain? Who's the lead flight attendant? The mother's name?"

Answers were relayed by radio, then by telephone.

"And the mother is Mrs. what?" he demanded.

There was an ominous silence.

"Miss? What do you mean, Miss?" he blurted. A cold chill crept up his back.

"Well, I'll get back to you if there's anything more," he told the wire service reporter. And, he did.

He suggested the wire service get the rest of the story from the paramedics or the hospital.

HOLLOW VICTORY

Like many fellow professionals, the public relations director of one of the nation's largest banks wishes there were times he could muzzle some of his colleagues.

Several years ago, he recalls, when the Japanese revalued the yen, the news broke early in the day.

An enterprising business editor for a major wire service called his next-door neighbor, the bank's chief economist, for comment, catching the latter at breakfast.

"It's great," the economist responded. "It's a victory for America. It means the U.S. economic plan is working."

Within an hour, the economist's reaction had been carried worldwide to the wire service's 4,000 subscribers.

When the public relations director arrived at his office, he was summoned to the chairman's office. Immediate "damage control" was demanded. The chief economist had neglected to remember some of the bank's most important clients were Japanese firms and the bank had a joint venture with a major Japanese financial institution. Rubbing salt in an open wound was not only indiscreet, it could affect future relationships.

By the time the bank's chairman started getting telephone calls from Tokyo, a more moderate comment had been drafted. But the public relations director was never sure the damage had been entirely undone.

WRITING SAMPLES

The director of communications for a health services organization in Honolulu has a favorite story about the credentials of a job applicant.

When an opening for a junior staff position was advertised, she relates, applicants were asked to submit a resumé and several writing samples.

One hopeful submitted a resumé which indicated three years of public relations experience. Attached to it was a sheet of ruled paper on which the applicant had carefully, and in a variety of styles of penmanship, written his name repeatedly down the page.

Unfortunately, despite the quality of his penmanship, those weren't the type of "writing samples" she had in mind.

3-ALLE

EDITORIAL JUDGMENT

The editor of a small daily newspaper tormented his state's largest utility company during the late 1930's with a constant barrage of critical, and often unfair, articles and editorials.

The company asked its public relations consultant to meet with the editor. The two men had been acquaintances, if not friends for at least a decade.

"I have nothing against your client," the editor told him. "In fact, I'd like to serve as a consultant for $50 a week. Some additional income would help with my wife's medical expenses. She has cancer."

The public relations consultant was shocked, but practical. He reported the conversation to his client.

"That's blackmail," exclaimed the utility's president.

"I think we should do it, however," the consultant said. "He was honest with me and we know he's having a hard time, even though his proposition is completely unethical."

The editor became a consultant on the public relations firm's payroll, and the latter was reimbursed by the utility. The critical articles and editorials ceased.

When the editor's wife died, he duly resigned his consultancy and never asked for anything further.

HIGH FLIGHT

During the nation's bicentennial, a Michigan public relations counselor assisted a prominent restaurateur with a salute to the nation's birthday and an attempt for a new record in the *Guinness Book of Records.*

The client's hobby was kite flying, so he planned to launch 1,776 kites and fly them on a single line. Teams would launch 100 kites at a time, then join the lines on a specially-built winch mounted on a pick-up truck. Reporters and photographers from two newspapers were on hand, as were crews from three television stations. The attempt promised to be a lot of fun and generate considerable publicity.

The first hundred kites rose in the air . . . then dropped into the river. Another hundred kites rose into the air . . . then dropped into the river. The weather simply would not cooperate. Wind conditions were too changeable and gusty for the kites to rise. The attempt had to be abandoned.

Fortunately, the client, being a restaurateur and a gracious host, had arranged for outdoor barbecue grills, plenty of refreshments and a Dixieland band.

While the record remained unbroken, the public relations counselor recalls everyone had a splendid time and the press coverage, which was extensive, wasn't in the least unkind, but highly entertaining.

GOOD LISTENERS

A public relations consultant with broadcast experience decided to offer media training seminars to his clients, several of which signed up promptly.

He walked into his first seminar to find not only a dozen participants, but several observers in the back of the room. The participants introduced themselves. The observers did not.

As the day went by, participants were interviewed on videotape and critiqued. The observers took copious notes and whispered to each other. At lunch they sat by themselves.

Finally the one-day workshop ended and the observers revealed who they were when one introduced herself.

"We're from corporate training and development. We were sent here as observers to make sure your seminar meets our corporate standards of educational philosophy, techniques and effectiveness."

Then she added more bluntly, "We were here to pull the plug on you if things hadn't gone as well as they did." The consultant has always wondered what educational philosophy and techniques have to do with coming out ahead on a live television interview. Knowledge and a good performance are what count under the lights in front of a live microphone.

BUSMAN'S HOLIDAY

Dealing with corporate management on one hand and the working press on the other often poses dilemmas.

The public relations director of Chicago company recalls a time he tried to do the right thing, but someone was bound to be unhappy in any event.

His firm had developed a new process for preserving fresh fruit which was being demonstrated in Washington State. His troubles began when a reporter for the *Wall Street Journal* visited his family's nearby farm during his annual vacation. Naturally, he got wind of the project.

When he called the company's headquarters, there was panic in the executive suite. Management wanted a clear competitive lead when ready to go to market.

After a long conversation and some pleading, the reporter agreed to delay a story on condition he would be given at least a one day advantage over other newspapers.

When approval to announce the process came, an advance copy was delivered to the *Journal's* bureau a day ahead of those distributed to other newspapers and magazines.

Management was happy. The reporter had beaten the competition. However, several business editors kept the public relations director's phone busy. They were not happy.

CHANNEL SURFING

The public relations director of a community college was assigned by its president to represent the school on the board of a new public television station.

He was promptly named co-chairman for a capital campaign and prepared a presentation on the station's needs.

With his co-chairman, a local banker, he made their first call on the chief executive officer of a large corporation headquartered in the city. After some initial chit-chat, he started his presentation.

Gradually he began to realize the executive, who'd evidenced interest at first, seemed puzzled. The public relations director paused for questions.

"If there's anything I've covered that isn't clear, perhaps I can explain?"

"Well, yes. There is," the chairman answered. "You keep mentioning Channel 27. I believe my set only goes up to 13."

The chagrined public relations director had to explain about UHF. He resisted an urge to tell the wealthy executive it had been several years since TV sets which could only receive VHF signals had been off the market.

A week later, the chairman pledged $20,000. The public relations director hoped he also planned to replace his set.

TUNNEL VISION

Early in his career, a public relations counselor recalls, he was responsible for press relations and community relations for a West Coast utility.

Much of his employer's hydroelectric power was produced by waters of the Colorado River passing through the turbines of Boulder Dam on the Arizona-Nevada border at Lake Mead.

One of his duties was to accompany press tours through tunnels carved out of solid rock to reach the penstock area above the 17 generators. It was often claustrophobic several hundred feet below the top of the dam, and most groups moved silently towards the daylight above.

On one occasion, however, he remembers a young reporter from California with a superficial knowledge of the region's geology.

"What would happen," he asked, "if an earthquake collapsed the tunnel?"

The public relations director didn't have a ready answer to that, but the young engineer who'd guided many such groups through the dam did.

"You'd all have to dig like crazy because there's another tour due through here in 30 minutes!"

PASSING THE BUCK

A junior public affairs staffer at a government agency in the nation's capital learned from his military experience that it's never wise to present a stationary target.

He usually arrived at work earlier than most of his colleagues, as did some of the top officials in the agency.

One morning about 6:30 a.m., the second highest official in the agency, a presidential appointee, stormed into his tiny office waving a copy of the *Washington Post*. He was fuming.

"Call the sonofabitch who wrote that story and tell him I never want to see anything like that in his paper again," he barked. The story hadn't been very flattering to say the least and contained some unattributed criticisms.

After the official spun on his heels and charged out of the office, the staffer took a deep breath as his heart rate returned to normal. Just then, his new boss, the director of public affairs, entered through another door.

"Was that who I think it was?" he inquired.

"Yes, sir." The staffer squeaked.

"What did he want?"

Unsure as to how to handle this minor crisis himself, he seized the opportunity.

"Well, sir, he was here to tell me you have a problem."

NEW BUSINESS

One of the partners in a Texas public relations firm frequently joined other professionals after work at a nearby pub. One evening, he held a long conversation with a local attorney who was duly impressed with the interesting projects on which the partner had worked in recent weeks. He admitted he'd never realized how effectively an attorney and a public relations practitioner might serve a client by working together.

Later in the week, the public relations counselor, unable to recall the attorney's name, asked one of his colleagues who he was with the intention of setting up a luncheon date. That afternoon, he called to extend an invitation, then made a reservation at a favorite restaurant.

When the attorney was escorted to his table, he realized immediately the attorney was a complete stranger. His colleague had given him the name of the wrong attorney and the wrong law firm. However, the luncheon turned out to be an unqualified success and resulted in several useful business leads.

The public relations counselor still tells the story on himself at seminars and workshops as an example of how he overcame his fear of making cold calls on prospective clients.

3-ALLE

PRIME TIME

A network television camera crew had been tipped off by dissident unionists that they planned to demonstrate in the New York offices of a leading oil company.

Several members of the company's public relations staff were deployed before the crew arrived, however, and were successful in keeping the two groups separated.

When some of the demonstrators appeared at the end of a hallway, the crew's cameraman asked what they were doing.

"They've handed out a few leaflets," was the reply.

"Well, that's not worth filming," the cameraman said as he headed for the elevator. "I don't see much of a story in that."

As the elevator doors closed, he leaned towards one of the company's public relations staff.

"By the way, my dad worked at your Oklahoma refinery for almost 40 years. Good luck."

JON. L. ALLEN

HOME SWEET HOME

A large suburban housing development was suddenly in serious trouble. Along one side of its 600 acres, houses had been built close to an ugly, foul-smelling dumpsite. Prospective buyers hadn't been warned beforehand.

The developer's public relations counsel was assured there was no problem, but homeowners told a different story. Protest signs appeared as well as articles in local media.

The builder, public relations counsel and attorneys held two days of rancorous meetings. Legal counsel urged a strong stand and libel suits against the media. They were adamantly opposed to public relations counsel's suggestion to buy back 18 homes and demolish them to make was for a protective greenbelt.

Some time later, after the public relations counsel had resigned the account, the attorneys were forced to defend several consolidated class action suits. Eventually, the issue was settled out of court with the builder being forced to buy back 171 homes and pay the plaintiffs' expenses.

A few years later, the public relations counsel was called by a former executive at the developer, now with another firm. He was offered a new account.

"Your integrity means as much to me as your ability," the new client explained.

.LE

FOREIGN AFFAIR

The public relations manager of an industrial firm in New England was assigned to help out at a trade show in Montreal. He invited a former secretary to accompany him on the trip.

The first evening in Montreal, he selected an obscure restaurant in the old quarter as the ideal place for dinner. It was secluded and not even mentioned in tourist guides, he was assured by a Canadian friend.

As the couple was ushered to their table, the owner seated them directly across the room from the public relations manager's chief executive officer. Neither acknowledged the other's presence during the evening, but the manager anticipated a reckoning when the trade show was over.

His first day back at his office, he was summoned by the chief executive officer. His boss got right to the point.

"Was that lady I saw with you in Montreal your wife?"

"No, sir, it wasn't," he answered, expecting his career to end abruptly.

"Good," replied the chief executive officer. "You know we have a firm company policy against taking wives on business trips."

AUDIENCE REACTION

After publication of his first book, the chairman of a Los Angeles public relations firm received an invitation to be a dinner speaker at a booksellers' convention. He sought advice from a local bookstore manger.

Since most bookstores are small businesses, the manager suggested the audience would be interested in some tips on how public relations and promotion might help improve business. He prepared his talk carefully, expecting rapt attention.

To his dismay, the audience hardly paid any attention. They continued talking, never realized when he'd finished and the only applause came from the others on the dais.

He asked a number of acquaintances who had been in the audience why the speech had been a failure.

"You blew it," one of them told him. "These people are out for an evening of fun. They're looking for laughs, not advice. Your firm represents many stars in the entertainment world and you mention several of them in your book.

"They wanted to hear funny stories about their favorites, especially the ones you didn't include in the book."

The chairman learned from the experience to seek advice from more than one person, especially those who'd attended similar events of the same type.

SITTING PRETTY

Sometimes using one's head is not the best way to resolve a situation. That was the conclusion of a public relations executive with a leading computer manufacturer.

He was called upon to attend a press conference on the West Coast at which his firm would demonstrate a new system slated for use in a government research project.

However, there was a major problem. The printer console contained an important feature still a closely-guarded trade secret. He was warned that, under no circumstances, could he allow any press people to see the new element or watch it in operation.

He pointed out to company headquarters in New York this would be difficult, since some 30 journalists would be roaming about the hall. He was told that was his problem, and headquarters was sure he'd be able to handle it.

After the press conference he stationed himself next to the printer, attempting to look nonchalant. All seemed to be going well. An experienced reporter from Electronic News sauntered over. The public relations man's mouth was dry, his heartbeat a little faster. He made an instant decision.

He climbed on the printer and sat on it. In that position, he had a cordial conversation with the reporter who then moved on, none the wiser.

DOMESTIC TRANQUILITY

Seasoned public relations professionals frequently get letters and calls from young hopefuls about entering the profession. Many such aspirants often have unusual ideas about the necessary qualifications, especially if they have limited work experience.

The editor of one of the oldest newsletters serving the public relations profession also reports receiving similar requests for advice and assistance.

One young man who reached her by phone was insistent he was particularly well-qualified for a career in public relations, despite the fact he was not familiar with what such duties might entail.

"Why are you so certain you're highly qualified?" the editor asked. The response was a classic she's treasured ever since.

"Because my mother-in-law has lived with us for seven years and we've never had an argument."

EXCLUSIVE INTERVIEW

A public relations counselor in the Middle West has found most journalists have high ethical standards. But one incident several years ago taught him that influential columnists can be exceedingly contrary.

While arranging a series of interviews in a small city for the president of a large corporation, his first call, 30 days in advance, was to such a columnist. The latter insisted on an exclusive interview, so the counselor consented, though he had other excellent contacts there.

Several days prior to the interview, the counselor called to confirm the appointment, which was set for 9 a.m.

In order to arrive on time, the client caught a 7 a.m. flight and arranged for a car and driver to take him to the columnist's office.

While his client was in flight, the columnist called to say he'd changed his mind. He'd found a better interview for his column that day.

The counselor was livid. His client was flying to the city for no other reason than an exclusive interview which the columnist had insisted upon. No other arrangements had been made in the belief they wouldn't be necessary.

The columnist indeed canceled, arrogantly and quite unconcerned with the inconvenience and expense he'd caused.

TOTAL RECALL

A highly-regarded public relations consultant served a stint early in his career as a speech writer at a major insurance company. The firm's president was difficult to please. He accepted every speech grudgingly, pleading that it was less than adequate. However, he consistently asked that his speeches be reprinted in booklet form and published in all three of the company's magazines.

Some years later, having started his own firm, the consultant landed his first major client. But he was less than happy to learn his former boss was an outside director of the company. He immediately feared he'd be exposed as "that public relations man who writes terrible speeches."

Shortly afterwards, the chairman of his new client called. "Jim,' he said, "our directors are meeting for dinner at my apartment tonight. I want them to meet you."

As the consultant arrived at an elegant building on upper Park Avenue, a limousine drew to the curb. Out stepped his former boss and his wife. Although a decade had passed, he walked directly over to his former speech writer.

Turning to his wife, he said, "Darling, this is the clever young man who used to write those wonderful speeches for me."

VINTAGE YEAR

A series of press tours arranged by a New York public relations counselor many years ago proved highly popular; although, there were some occasional surprises.

Each year, four or five newspaper columnists were invited to tour the Charente region of France not far from Bordeaux. One highlight of the tour was an elegant dinner at an historic chateau owned by a distinguished titled family.

The meal was served by two red-jacketed waiters — one for the food and one for the different wines which accompanied each of the five courses.

As the wine waiter leaned forward to pour each wine, he murmured the name of its vintage and year.

A Chicago-based syndicated columnist who was a member of that year's tour heard the waiter announce, "Chateau Cheval Blanc '53."

The columnist, who'd fortified himself for the evening with several shots form his flask of bourbon, staggered to his feet and raised his glass in response.

"Purdue '52!"

STRAY TYPE

As the governor of a Southern state neared completion of his second term, his friends and supporters arranged a testimonial dinner. A local public relations firm prepared news releases and helped him draft his remarks.

The morning after the big event, the firm's president received a call from the editor of a large newspaper. The latter went to great pains to explain how newspapers are produced, almost starting with how trees are turned into pulp, then newsprint. At the time, copy was still set on linotype machines, so he explained that on very, very rare occasions, a block of type from one article might be mixed in with that from another by accident.

"You mean you screwed up?" the public relations man asked. The editor was reluctant to admit it, but confessed that was the case.

The story about the testimonial dinner started out fine, but right in the middle was a paragraph from a wire service story about the racketeering trial of a prominent labor leader. It cited a conspiracy involving government witnesses.

The hapless governor received several calls asking about his relationship with the defendant. Fortunately, his second term was drawing to a close and he took the matter quite lightly and was savvy enough to understand the error.

LE

DIPLOMATIC IMMUNITY

A public relations counselor numbered among her favorite clients an elegant restaurant in suburban Virginia, just a few minutes from the nation's capital.

On one occasion, the restaurant's manager alerted her that U.S. State Department security people had informed him that a "principal" planned to have lunch there on a certain Thursday. During the three previous days, she and the manager watched with fascination as agents wearing earphones and using two-way radios checked out the dining room, kitchen, restrooms and every corner of the premises.

When Thursday arrived, a sense of excitement was evident in the air. Precisely at noon, the State Department security team swept into the restaurant, taking three tables. None of the guests looked the slightest bit familiar or resembled anyone pictured in local newspapers that week.

Finally, after the meal, one of the party of 12 rose to pay the bill. She thanked the manager for his hospitality and cooperation, explaining the group had been conducting a State Department training exercise.

He was somewhat disappointed the occasion hadn't been newsworthy, but he underestimated his public relations counselor. Her version of the training exercise scenario appeared the following day as the lead story in the Style section of the *Washington Post*.

LAW ENFORCEMENT

The civilian who handled press relation for the police department in a small New England city thought she'd come up with an outstanding idea for the local newspaper.

When the department acquired its first patrol dog, she arranged for a photograph of the city's chief of police shaking the canine recruit's paw. The caption indicated the German Shepherd was a welcome addition to the force. As the photograph was posed, it included the chief, the dog and the dog's handler, properly identified from left to right.

However, when it appeared in the newspaper, the news desk had cropped out the handler and deleted his name from the caption, so it could run in a vertical rather than a horizontal space.

She received a lot of kidding from friends in the department because, with only two figures now in the photo, the chief was still identified as the one at the left. She was congratulated on the accuracy of the caption, lest readers not recognize which was the chief and which was the German Shepherd.

ON TARGET

A public relations professional can often define and solve a problem better than a client or, for that matter, an old friend unversed in effective communications.

A consultant in the Middle West recalls when a friend was attempting to market bus tours covering several thousand miles during the era before air travel became commonplace.

His announcements, sent to daily newspapers, were either not used or relegated to back pages of Sunday travel sections. After receiving few responses, he voiced his frustration to the public relations consultant.

The latter suggested he stop wasting his effort on a general readership, but target his message to persons who normally have summer vacations of three or more weeks — namely teachers.

The result was a news story about the tours, written with the interests of teachers in mind and published in the next edition of the state education association's newsletter.

Although it was late in the season, enough teachers responded that several bus tours were sold out. The tour operator still regards his friend as a genius, but all the latter did was target the right product to the right audience.

JON. L. ALLEN

SCREEN PASS

A Tennessee public relations counselor has delivered news releases by mail, courier, wire, fax and in person, but there was one occasion that was absolutely unique. At the time, he was public relations director for a university.

He was alone in the school's locked administration building late one Saturday night when two security officers appeared and asked if anyone else was in the building.

"Not that I know of," he answered. "There was a meeting here about an hour ago, but I think they've all gone."

"Five minutes ago a motorcycle drove up outside," said one of the officers. "The driver honked and a large envelope sailed out of a third floor window. Do you know anything about it?"

Earlier in the evening, the president of the university had decided to announce the appointment of a new athletic director prior to leaving on vacation. He'd summoned all the coaches to his office at 7:30 p.m.

With a number of phone calls to make, the public relations director had telephoned the sports editor of the city's major newspaper to explain his dilemma. He couldn't leave his office and access to the building was impossible.

The sports editor, who considered it a major story and wanted to carry it Sunday morning, had sent the motorcyclist to pick up the news release and a photograph.

LE

A QUIET PLACE

The public relations manager of a new luxury hotel in Asia had been assigned an office in which he was easily distracted by the high noise level. The solution to his problem, he decided, would be an acoustical ceiling, but the government levied steep duty charges on imported building materials.

Fortunately, because the hotel was new, it had been selected as a convention site by an international travel organization.

The manager solved his problem by ordering more than enough ceiling tiles for his office. They passed through customs duty-free when he explained they were merely small bulletin boards he planned to place throughout the hotel and were essential for posting notices, daily schedules and messages during the forthcoming convention.

When the conventioneers had departed, the hotel's maintenance staff collected them, and the public relations manager had his acoustical ceiling.

JON. L. ALLEN

ABOVE AND BEYOND

Besides being asked to get engagement and wedding announcements published, public relations professionals are asked occasionally to arrange for glowing obituaries. One public relations executive recalls an especially difficult assignment. One of his firm's senior executives asked him to arrange for an obituary in the *New York Times* for a sister who had spent her entire working life as the underpaid legal counsel for a major charity.

He gathered as much information as he could, then called the metropolitan desk hoping he might be able to get an inch or two on the obit page. Much to his surprise, he was connected with a reporter he knew who was filling in on the desk that day.

"I know who you're talking about," the reporter exclaimed. "My wife went to school with her. She was one of the most remarkable, generous people we've ever known."

Her obituary ran 10 inches as the lead story on the obit page the following day and contained details about her life about which he'd been unaware.

As a result, the public relations executive's reputation rose immeasurably in his company's executive suite, and he certainly wasn't foolish enough to reveal how he accomplished extraordinary feats with the press.

MANAGEMENT INFORMATION

At many corporations, the public relations staff prepares news summaries for senior executives. Often, the stories are ones which appeared in out-of-town newspapers, trade journals or foreign publications not ordinarily read.

Just such a service was provided at a large petroleum company at the request of a former chairman of the board. The source of each item was credited and the original was placed in the corporate library. For several years, the service received only favorable comments.

One morning, the editor received a call from a senior vice president who was obviously distressed. Apparently, a story in which the company was mentioned contained an error. He was chided for not checking its accuracy.

The story he'd summarized had appeared in a respected business journal published in Asia, but the senior vice president told him he should check the accuracy of every item he used, some 30 each week, more than 1,500 a year, even though the summaries were circulated internally only.

However, he never had an opportunity. Within a few days, the company's new chief executive officer instructed that the service be discontinued completely. Apparently the possibility of another error by a journalist on the other side of the world outweighed the value of keeping the company's management informed.

　　　　JON. L. ALLEN

SILVER SCREEN

Among the prominent guests attending the premiere of a corporate film in Washington, D.C. was a senior cabinet minister from the country in which the film had been produced.

Visibly impressed, he spoke at length with the executive hosting the premiere and reception. Since he would be returning to his country in a few days, the minister offered any assistance the company might require there.

The executive seized the opportunity to mention more than $2 million in blocked dividends which the company was unable to convert into hard currency. The minister offered to look into the matter.

Some months later, the funds were released, despite the country's continued shortage of foreign exchange, and the executive learned that a certain cabinet minister had been responsible.

When the company's senior management became aware of the circumstances, its public relations manager seldom heard any objections to any proposals for new films in the company's highly-regarded international film program.

LE

GOOD MILEAGE

A talented automotive writer with a wide readership was a colorful college drop-out who dominated his field in the years following World War II.

By the 1960s, his eminence was so established he retired to Florida. From there, he demanded, with little objection, that any auto makers seeking to have their products "road tested" and reviewed had to deliver them to his beach home.

One year, the public relations manager at a major auto maker was particularly pleased with his glowing report on a new model, written in his amusing, rambling style. His article was accompanied by several excellent photographs in which an attractive model appeared.

He was surprised, therefore, when he received a call from his company's zone manager in Florida. The latter reported that when the car was picked up at the writer's home, it had the same mileage on the odometer it had when it was delivered.

A more careful look at the photographs revealed they'd all been cleverly posed in the writer's driveway.

At least this time, the public relations manager knew where the car was! On a previous occasion, the writer had left another model in an airport parking lot several hundred miles from his home and forgotten which one.

ENCHANTED EVENING

In the early days of television, before it was possible to videotape ahead of time, local political candidates often appeared live. One such candidate with a reputation for consuming quantities of bourbon purchased 15 minutes of air time. His press aide was unable to give the station manager a copy of his remarks. He planned to ad lib them.

They were in a quandary. Federal Communications Commission rules did not permit any interruptions or censorship, but stations were held responsible for any profanity on the air.

The evening of the broadcast, the candidate indeed fortified himself with several shots of his favorite beverage. He delivered his message as scheduled with less anxiety than anticipated, despite several obscenities. When it was over, he called his family to find out how he'd looked and, reassured, thanked the station's staff for a good show.

He never did learn what the station manager, press aide and his own family had conspired to do. He'd spoken into a dead microphone while the sound track of a current Broadway musical had been all viewers heard as he faced the camera.

3-ALLE

CAMPUS CAPER

During the 1960's, the chairman of a public relations firm in the Southwest was director of public relations for a major university. At the time, marijuana was in wide use among young people.

One day, the local afternoon newspaper, in reporting a drug bust near the campus, actually proclaimed in the headline the raid had occurred at the university. The director of public relations rushed into the city to set the record straight with the managing editor, an old friend.

The latter was somewhat reluctant to admit any error until it was pointed out to him that several retail stores were actually closer to his newsroom than the location of the drug raid was to university property. He agreed he'd never condone a headline which implied a nearby crime had occurred on the newspaper's premises when in fact it had not.

The editor referred the university spokesman to the headline writer, an alumnus of the university who'd spent a summer internship working for the public relations director. He was most apologetic and promised a correction in the next edition.

True to his word, he wrote a correction which carried another headline. However, it caused his former boss to give up in frustrations.

It read: "Drug Bust at University Has No School Ties."

HOT COPY

When a former newsman with more than 30 years experience at a major wire service joined the news bureau at an Ivy League university, he saw no reason to modify his writing style.

After his first few months on the job, he received a derisive memo about the news releases he'd written from an especially pretentious vice president in the school's administration. His new releases, it was suggested, read too much like "wire service stories."

This troubled him at first.

He thought perhaps he should adapt his way of telling a story to what would please his academic colleagues rather than what would capture editors' attention.

He consulted several former colleagues, and one told him he couldn't have received a finer compliment. He reminded him that generations of wire service reporters had been told by editors to "write it for the milkman in Kansas City."

Since he hadn't heard any criticism from editors and his news releases were always well-received, he continued writing them just as he'd been trained.

LE

POWER PLAY

A trade association public affairs executive in Ohio found it necessary to apologize to a member of his board of directors for an error in one of the organization's publications.

The volunteer board member, an executive at a large power company, remained critical of the association's staff.

"In our company, an error such as that would have been impossible. We have two full-time people who proofread every document to avoid making even a single mistake."

The public affairs executive's staff consisted of himself and one assistant, but he accepted responsibility for the error.

"We don't have such resources available to us. Such a level of service must cost a great deal?"

"Not at all," the power company executive responded airily. "It doesn't cost us anything. They're already on staff."

That stumped the public affairs director, but whenever he's told of the encounter since, always adds, "I remember that every time I pay my utility bill."

HORSING AROUND

One of those individuals who own a token number of shares in several companies always attended their corporate annual meetings and asked tough questions.

At one corporation in the Middle West, his arrival was invariably a source of distress for the public relations director, but he could do little other than make sure his chief executive officer was well-prepared.

One year the visitor appeared as expected and rose to ask several questions. The chairman handled them skillfully and there was an almost audible sigh of relief in the room.

Another regular attendee rose to congratulate the questioner for his efforts for shareholders in general. He praised him more than anyone thought necessary, concluding that he was serving American business extremely well as a corporate "gadfly."

Just then, one of the corporation's elderly directors, seated in the front row, turned to make a comment to his neighbors. As he spoke, the sound level in the room dropped so most of the audience could hear him.

"Gadfly, eh! Isn't that an insect that hovers around a horse's rump?"

The questioner never attended that particular company's annual meetings again.

DÉJÀ VU

A corporate magazine editor researched and wrote an article for his company's publication which was so good, he earned several compliments including a handwritten note from his boss.

Other corporate magazine editors subsequently requested permission to reprint the article with credit, of course.

Several months later, he received through company mail a copy of his article reprinted in another publication. Attached was a note from his boss who'd written, "Why don't we run something like this in our magazine?" Obviously he'd missed the credit line at the end of the article.

Anxious not to embarrass his boss, the editor pulled a copy of the original article from the files, attached his boss' note and added a memo in response: "I suggest we not use an article on this subject because it's very similar to the attached which appeared in our magazine last year."

The editor's boss responded with another handwritten note. "Thanks for being diplomatic about my failing memory."

ORIGINAL RESEARCH

A public relations educator often does some consulting for a large corporation. On one occasion, he was asked to conduct a survey of financial analysts to learn what type of information they wanted from the parent company and its various subsidiaries.

The answer came back loud and clear. Analysts wanted less from the chairman and more from other executives. As might be expected from someone with his ego, the chairman was displeased. "Who is the fellow who did this?" he asked his vice president of public relations.

"He's a professor at a major university with a doctorate in research."

"Never heard of him," the chairman said. "Get someone who knows what he's doing." As a result, the vice president retained a large national firm to conduct the same research at ten times the original cost.

The findings were virtually identical.

When the vice president apologized to the educator for his chairman's reaction, he added: "Don't let it worry you. If we hadn't commissioned your survey first, he'd never have let me spend that much money on the other one."

LE

UNAUTHORIZED VERSION

When he reported to his company's general counsel some years ago, the public relations director of a manufacturing company could never fathom the workings of a legal mind.

On several occasions, articles unfavorable to the company appeared in major newspapers. Invariably, he was called on the carpet and blamed. After all, the lawyer reasoned, only the public relations director could have been responsible for unauthorized disclosures. In a number of instances, the revelations were news even to the public relations director.

What he knew, and the general counsel never understood, was that the company was a favorite target of a single issue, special interest lobbying organization in the nation's capital with access to considerable information in the public domain and a sophisticated, self-serving publicity operation. The organization was well-financed and adept at courting national media.

Eventually, the public relations director concluded the general counsel needed a scapegoat so he wouldn't become one himself. After the public relations director and the lawyer both retired, the former's successor reported to another vice president. Fortunately, that vice president had worked briefly for a wire service after graduating from college and had a better understanding of the "real world."

JON. L. ALLEN

CONTROLLED DISTRIBUTION

When a stunningly attractive employee of a Texas financial institution won a local beauty contest, an article and photograph in the organization's newsletter was a must. And, a highly popular, albeit opinionated and entertaining newspaper columnist, who'd served as a judge for the contest, agreed to write the story as a favor to the organization's public relations director.

His article, for which he expected no fee, was amusing and the photo of the contest winner was a real eye-catcher.

After more than 1,000 copies of the newsletter had been printed, the organization's president instructed the public relations director to destroy them. Fearsome of the consequences and the potential for unfavorable publicity, the public relations director protested without success.

Less than two weeks later, the newspaper columnist retaliated. He told his 300,000 readers the president was a "jerkola" and a tyrant and blasted him for his censorship.

Moreover, he offered a photocopy of the article he "doesn't want you to read" to any reader who sent him a stamped, self-addressed envelope. Not only did several hundred of the organization's employees respond, but so did many other readers, prompted by simple curiosity.

IN THE PICTURE

A senior Air Force public affairs officer was often called upon to provide guidance to local public affairs officers at the 15 bases in his command.

"The boss is driving me crazy," the public affairs officer at one base reported. "He wants his picture in the base newspaper every week, and my editor is furious."

The more experienced officer came up with a plan for his local staffer. Each week the commander would visit workers on the job.

The first photograph depicted him talking to security police guards at 3 a.m. in subfreezing weather. Next he visited mess hall cooks before breakfast, then mechanics working on an aircraft engine, then medical technicians in the base clinic. Each caption included comments about what the men and women liked and disliked about their work.

At first the commander didn't think much of the idea, especially the late night and early morning sessions. He saw its potential, however, and went along, eventually becoming quite enthusiastic about the series.

The series became one of the best read features in the base newspaper and its editor received calls suggesting new locations. As might have been expected, the commander became quite popular.

NOTHING VENTURED

The president of an independent oil company assigned his public relations counsel to prepare a presentation for a group of potential investors. Rather than give the counsel's staff a free hand, he meddled almost daily, convinced of his own "better" ideas. At the end of two weeks, everyone was thoroughly confused and there'd been little progress.

The president called everyone together for a meeting and talked without pause for two hours about what he wanted. Finally, the presentation was completed and everyone was pleased, much to their surprise. The following week, the president flew to Tulsa to make the presentation.

On his return, he called his public relations counsel. "Well, I made the damn presentation," he said sarcastically. "The investors walked out without a word when it was over."

The next day, the public relations counsel received a phone call from the oilman's secretary. She'd overheard his comments.

"Those deadbeats walked out because they couldn't come up with 10 bucks between them," she said. "They were real phonies. It's a wonderful presentation. Everyone really likes it. He just won't admit it."

CUTTING EDGE

Plans were being set for the opening of a new 350-bed university hospital to replace an existing facility. First, it was decided to hold a formal dedication and conduct a tour before the patients were transferred.

"Who should cut the ribbon?" the school's president asked his public relations director.

"Why not our most senior employee?" The president liked the suggestion, and the hospital's personnel department identified an x-ray technician with 34 years of service. Since the hospital was associated with a medical school, she would wield a scalpel to snip the ribbon.

At the dedication, trustees and other dignitaries were lined up on the stairwell, a long yellow ribbon in front of them. As spectators craned their necks for a good view, photographers took their places.

Action! The president held the ribbon. The x-ray technician cut through it — right into the president's little finger. It was a minor incision, but the president had the distinction of becoming the emergency room's first patient.

The public relations director lay low for a few days. But local press coverage was sensational, he recalls.

ON THE WATERFRONT

A dozen years ago, a consultant now on the West Coast secured a "dream" job as public relations director of a cruise line which offered several Caribbean voyages a year.

The arrival of her company's newest liner in New York was delayed several times. Finally, two months later than planned, the ship was at sea. She set up a welcome ceremony, revised the press kits and invited print and broadcast media. Even though interest had understandably waned during the delays, it was fortunately a slow news day.

Just as she was congratulating herself while the ship maneuvering in the Hudson River near its berth, a stowaway escaped from custody below deck, rushed to the bow and jumped into the harbor in full view of reporters and cameramen.

Needless to say, the liner's arrival made the news, but the stowaway received more coverage than the welcoming ceremony. It did serve to draw attention to the ship and the fact the stowaway had selected it for his voyage.

Shortly after, the public relations director resigned to accept another post. She never admitted to her previous employer she was subject to seasickness anyway.

SILENT SOLUTION

Assigned to write his company's college recruiting brochure some years ago, a public relations manager studied previous editions and noticed each contained a stilted letter from the chairman of the board, yet lacked what he considered essential information.

By coincidence, Opinion Research Corporation had recently completed a survey of college seniors, evaluating recruiting brochures. Of 32 items rated, a chairman's letter ranked dead last.

Emboldened, he proposed replacing the letter with a table of contents, but his superior bridled at the suggestion. He'd never endorse something which might be construed as disrespectful of the chairman.

The following year, the public relations manager solved his dilemma. He dropped the letter in favor of a table of contents and submitted the brochure for approval several days prior to the company's annual meeting. It was approved without comment.

The moral he draws is even the most sensible proposal can be doomed by drawing attention to it. The best tactic is to keep one's mouth shut and simply do it.

MAJORITY RULE

The director of public affairs for a trade association devoted many months to developing a story for the *New York Times*. The local bureau manager even suggested how the group might secure a Sunday story which would make its membership proud.

The public affairs director drafted the association's first Code of Ethics, embodying the highest management principles. The executive committee endorsed it unanimously.

At the association's annual convention in Milwaukee, he was sure the 100-member board of directors would approve. The *New York Times* man even wrote the story in advance.

However, the public affairs director's board rejected the Code of Ethics by a vote of 97 to 3. They feared it might haunt them in labor negotiations.

"What do I do?" the *Times* man asked.

"Kill the story; tell the truth," the public affairs director responded.

Within a few days, several dozen chief executive officers were furious their representatives had rejected the Code of Ethics. It was a black eye for the association. The response of many of its directors was to demand the public affairs director be fired.

"Fire him now," the man from the *Times* told one of them. "And you'll get another story you'll like even less." The two remained good friends for many years.

LE

KITTY CITY

A film publicist and a theater manager in a small town came up with a novel promotion for a supernatural thriller about cats.

They scheduled a Saturday morning screening for kids, with anyone bringing a cat admitted free of charge.

When the day arrived, several hundred boys and girls stood in line, each holding an angry cat. It was obvious many of the patrons had not laid eyes on their "pets" more than a day or two before. As the felines were deposited in the lobby, the manager sent an usher out to buy several gallons of milk and several hundred paper bowls. Pandemonium was averted.

But smiles faded from their faces when the film ended. The crowd of youngsters streamed past them out of the theater, ignoring, for the most part, their "pets." Close to a hundred castaway felines were milling in the lobby, all howling at the top of their lungs. In desperation, the theater manager and his staff rounded up the cats, loaded them in a panel truck and headed for the town's main square. When they opened the doors, scores of cats leaped out, sprinting in every direction. Traffic was snarled until the last feline bailed out and headed down a nearby alley.

The publicist never returned to that town. Nor did he ever learn the fate of the unfortunate theater manager.

STUDIO SESSION

To secure photographs of his company's directors and officers for the annual report, the public relations director arranged for a photographer to set up his equipment in a room adjacent to the boardroom.

The session went smoothly as the photographer's attractive young assistant prepared each group for the shots.

The chairman of the board had been scheduled last. Several outside directors had flights to catch, and he was to be photographed by himself. He paced the floor impatiently, anxious to get on with the day's business.

When the time came for his sitting, the assistant started to prepare him. He muttered grumpily. "I don't want to do this, you know. I've more important things to do."

Unaware of his status in the company, the young assistant ran a comb through his hair and dabbed touches of makeup on his cheeks and chin. Then, as if speaking to one of her children, she adjusted his collar and necktie.

"We all have to do things we don't want to sometimes," she murmured. "This is one of them. So sit still, dear, and let's get on with it."

The chairman melted. He relaxed. He smiled. He was cooperative. Later, he had high praise for the photographs and even ordered additional prints for his personal use.

3-ALLE

SECRET MISSION

Thirty years ago, a major corporation built an exotic metals plant in a small Southern city. However, demand for its products eventually diminished, and the firm decided to seek a new use for the facility.

The corporation's vice president of public relations was summoned to the president's office. He was informed that several board members were flying to the plant city to meet their counterparts from a large steel company.

"We're going to discuss a joint venture, and we've agreed to keep the meeting secret. No statements."

The vice president was familiar with the city's only newspaper. He knew its editor had sources at the airport, hotels, private clubs and elsewhere. His newspaper also filed business stories with a wire service and dailies in New York and Chicago. He recommended, since the arrival of two corporate jets couldn't be hidden, a brief announcement of " preliminary discussions" might be prudent. No, he was told forcefully.

The next day, the newspaper headlined speculation that a joint venture was in the making. And, the story appeared in New York and Chicago.

The president summoned his public relations executive again. "You screwed that up!" he barked. "You were supposed to keep it out of the press."

JON. L. ALLEN

STAR PERFORMANCE

A television producer who once served as a military public affairs officer learned upon returning from overseas he was a candidate for a highly-coveted new assignment. The major general who commanded the organization always insisted on interviewing candidates in person.

A meeting was arranged. The young officer arrived promptly, entered the general's office and saluted. The general had a reputation as a tough boss and, as the young candidate looked at the two silver stars on each of the general's shoulders framing a face which might have been carved from granite, he felt some apprehension.

He found himself doing most of the talking as he summarized his experience for the commander. The latter absorbed everything wordlessly. Finally, he broke his silence with several questions. Just as the public affairs officer thought the interview was over, the general posed one final question.

"What will be your most important priority if you join this command?"

"To get you your third star, sir," the candidate shot back without hesitation.

"You're hired, captain. They can cut the orders later, but I want you on board as soon as possible."

LE

CONFLICT OF INTEREST

A senior partner in a major law firm in the Middle West called a prominent public relations counselor to request his assistance on a highly confidential crisis communications project which required immediate attention.

The law firm planned to dismiss one of its partners over the weekend, lock up his files and print new letterheads. Also needed were a news release announcing the action and letters to clients and employees of the law firm explaining the action. Since discretion was essential, all these had to be accomplished off the premises.

Everything went off perfectly, exactly as planned, by the time Monday morning arrived.

Then, just before noon, the public relations counselor received a telephone call from the partner who'd been ousted. He'd been advised by a close friend that he should retain public relations counsel to represent him, completely unaware of the latter's role over the weekend.

The counselor learned that the close friend who'd made the referral was one of his other clients, but he advised the lawyer politely that he already represented a local law firm and didn't feel he could accept a similar assignment.

DOG DAYS

After several years on the staff of a trade magazine, an editor accepted a post with a chemical company in New Jersey. He was unaware of the unusual tasks public relations staffers often handle beyond their normal duties.

Two weeks after he joined the firm, he was summoned to the office of a vice president for a "special project."

It turned out a family dog had just died and the vice president's family wanted to bury their faithful pet beside a favorite tree. The editor was asked to secure a suitable plaque to mount on the tree and to call the executive's wife for details.

When he called her, she started sobbing but managed to inform him the dog's name was Fluffie. She was able to provide him with the dates of Fluffie's birth and death, but she had no suggestions for the plaque. "How about 'In memory of a friend who will always be remembered?'" he suggested.

After he found a supplier willing to make the plaque, the latter posed another question: "What's the circumference of the tree?" He'd need that so he could curve the plaque properly. Another call to the distraught wife who made the necessary measurement with the tape from her sewing kit.

A "special project" completed and a bizarre introduction to the world of corporate public relations.

HARD NIGHT'S WORK

When the public relations director of a securities firm had lunch with a friend in the corporate lending department of a major bank, the latter asked, in a teasing way, "How do you p.r. types spend a typical day?"

Responding to the challenge, he answered facetiously, "I get to the office about 8 a.m., read my mail and try to come up with at least a couple of creative ideas, then meet a client for lunch. In the afternoon, I try to come up with a couple of more original ideas and always set aside a few hours for putting those ideas in writing."

"That's pretty much what I thought you do."

Late that same day, the public relations director received a frantic call from the trust department of his friend's bank. A truckload of annual reports and proxy statements had just been delivered shortly after the receiving clerks had left for the day. Since they had to be postmarked the following day, the public relations director rushed to the loading dock, rolled up the sleeves of his custom-made shirt and started unloading the shipment.

As he worked late that night he thought of his banker friend. Not only was he home sound asleep, but likely could not find his own mailroom if his job had depended on it.

THE UNINVITED

A public relations manager for a retail chain was responsible for seating at a company table whenever his management subscribed to banquet, charity ball or fund-raiser. He often had difficulty filling the table.

On one occasion, he had no problem. It was a gala evening with top entertainers contributing their talent to raise funds for a new hospital. Each table was priced at $25,000.

As he entered the ballroom, he encountered an executive from his company he hadn't invited, although he had on previous occasions. Visibly shaken, he was overcome by panic.

"What are you doing?" he asked. "There's no place for you at the table. For God's sake don't embarrass me." The executives he'd invited would see her when they arrived.

"You weren't expecting me?" She smiled. "I wouldn't miss this for anything. Who else is here from the company?"

He was becoming increasingly distraught, so she decided to ease his mind. Her husband, whom he'd met only once previously, was the public relations director of a very large multinational corporation and was hosting one of the best tables at the affair. That was where she expected to sit with the chief executive officer, his wife and other senior executives of her husband's company.

GREAT GHOST

Public relations staffers at a major corporation slaved over speeches for their president, invariably making revisions right up to the last hour. They were surprised, therefore, when he delivered an address at the dedication of the company's new office tower in New York without requesting any assistance from his public relations staff.

His remarks were brief, no more then ten minutes. Moreover, they were eloquent, graceful and deeply moving — absolutely appropriate to the occasion. The audience was transfixed and numerous requests were received for the text.

His public relations staff knew he couldn't have written the speech himself. He wasn't that articulate and he abhorred speaking in public.

Some inquiries by the company's public relations director revealed the chairman has asked a friend with whom he'd gone to college almost 50 years earlier to prepare his remarks for him. What a friend.

The ghostwriter of the president's remarkable text turned out to be the author of eighteen books, seven Broadway plays and a three-time winner of the Pulitzer Prize. At the time of his death 20 years later at the age of 90, the president's ghostwriter was one of America's most respected men of letters.

LANGUAGE BARRIER

A prominent aviation writer and his wife were co-editors and co-publishers of a highly-regarded aviation magazine published in the Republic of South Africa. They were frequent visitors to Europe and the United States.

On one such trip, following a working visit to a West Coast aircraft manufacturer, the company's public relations director hosted them for dinner at an elegant lakeside restaurant.

By the time after-dinner coffee was served, the sun had set and several neon lights across the lake were illuminated. The writer's wife glanced across the lake and burst into uncontrollable laughter. The public relations director asked her what she saw that was so amusing.

"That sign," she said. "The one advertising Grandma's Cookies. In our country a 'cookie' is a streetwalker."

SECOND OPINION

A public relations staffer at a Massachusetts hospital recalls once being in the position to make a difference in the life of a distraught widow.

Her husband, a despondent disabled veteran, attempted suicide and was rushed to the hospital. After several days in intensive care, he died of cardiac arrest.

The attending physician, a native of South Asia, listed the cause of death as "suicide." The wife, destitute and in a panic over the loss of her husband, learned she might lose his veteran's benefits. Confused and weeping, she sought the public relations staffer's help.

The foreign-born doctor balked at a suggestion he might have erred, but eventually relented. The death certificate was corrected to show cause of death as "cardiac arrest," quite proper inasmuch as he'd survived the suicide attempt and lived several more days.

She retained her benefits, received a burial allowance and preference for government employment.

Despite the physician's professional ability, he wasn't aware of all the circumstances. The public relations staffer believes it's always best to determine them before rushing to a decision.

JON. L. ALLEN

NIGHT GAME

New York publicists of an earlier generation, when there were as many as 14 newspapers in the city, could easily spend much of the day in a favorite tavern as reporters, editors, columnists or critics slipped in for drinks between visits to the newsroom.

One theatrical press agent whose working day started some time after noon recalls cultivating many of his best contacts this way.

On one occasion, he swears, a sportswriter with whom he was having a lively debate one afternoon left the bar, presumably to make a phone call.

Upon his return, he confessed he'd been to Philadelphia to cover a night game and had already filed his copy, before returning to the bar to pick up the debate.

The publicist hadn't moved during the six hours the reporter had been away.

LE

PHOTO OPPORTUNITIES

Shortly after the introduction of commercial jets, a new public relations staffer at a major airline fielded a call from a freelance writer who claimed numerous credits in major magazines.

Now, he explained, he'd been assigned to do a feature article on in-flight services for the business traveler and needed a selection of stock photos. Other airlines had been very helpful. The public relations staffer picked several from the files — flight attendants welcoming passengers at the cabin door, stowing overcoats, serving cocktails and distributing pillows and blankets.

When a copy of the article arrived from the airline's clipping service several months later, the public relations staffer felt a very long lunch hour to be in order. The article and photo captions dwelt on a theme of "sex in the sky" with the implication that the flight attendants were being more than helpful and, in fact, were propositioning business travelers.

Fortunately, the public relations staffer's superior, a retired admiral, had a wry sense of humor.

"We've been had." he exclaimed. "These things sometimes happen. Anyway, it might even be good for business."

SATISFACTION GUARANTEED

Negotiations for a corporate acquisition had been lengthy and complex. Then, to satisfy regulatory requirements, company management grudgingly agreed to an announcement as long as it was approved by legal counsel.

The company's public relations manager prepared a terse, factual one-page news release and submitted it for approval. When it was returned to him, it had grown to six pages, replete with disclaimers and technicalities.

"This will satisfy the stock exchange, the SEC and every agency that regulates our industry," one of the company's lawyers beamed. It probably did, but even the most experienced business editors, unable to grasp its awkward sentence structure and obscure language passed it up. Those who attempted to interpret it for their readers made several errors which only the company's lawyers noticed with glee.

Stockholders, financial analysts, portfolio managers, customers and suppliers flooded the company's switchboard with calls. The public relations manager had the satisfaction of referring every inquiry to the attorney who'd revised the announcement.

The one lesson the latter had learned at law school, apparently, was how to turn a simple, sensible statement into a complex, obscure, turgid document that only his classmates could possibly understand.

GOOD COPY

The business editor of a California newspaper conducted an interview with the executive vice president of a trade association. Despite the fact he asked good questions, the answers were evasive, bland and noncommittal.

The next day the editor called the association's public relations manager. "There's no story here," he said. "Can't you put something better together?" The public relations manager worked late to write a statement, covering everything he thought his boss *should* have said.

"Now that's good copy," the editor responded. "It's strong. It's solid news. But, I'd better read it to your boss to make sure he's willing to be quoted."

Surprisingly, he was. He told the editor it was just what had been on his mind, but that he'd had difficulty expressing it. After the story appeared, the executive received dozens of phone calls congratulating him on his strong stand on the issues.

The following day, he was admitted to a hospital with a mild nervous breakdown. His public relations manager was one of his first visitors.

"I suppose I can't take all this success at one time," he confided. "I'm not sure I can handle it. You've been a tremendous help. In fact, you express my positions on industry issues far better than I can. You deserve a big salary increase."

STOCK ANSWER

The president of a Los Angeles public relations firm which handles investor relations for several companies will never forget an incident which broke up a serious conference in peals of laughter.

While a particular client was being discussed, it was noted by an account supervisor that the company was an OTC firm. Rather than being listed on one of stock exchanges, its stock was traded over-the-counter.

As an afterthought, he turned to the most junior staff member in the meeting, a young woman who'd only been with the firm for a few weeks.

"Nancy, you know what OTC is, right?" She certainly did.

"Of course," the young staffer responded in all seriousness. "Out-of-the Country."

LE

AUTHOR, AUTHOR

The Chairman of The Board of the tire company was invited to address a business audience in a city in Ohio. Rather than trust the speech to an untested writer, he assigned it to his senior public relations executive. The remarks dealt with his personal growth as he rose to top management.

When the time came for him to speak, he strode to the podium and placed his text on the lectern.

"I am a humble man," he began, "who grows day by day as I manage people and assets. I believe it's important to recognize my colleagues for their accomplishments. For example, I am about to deliver remarks which I've not read, but I know they will be excellent because they were prepared by one of the finest professionals in our industry."

"Would he please stand and be recognized? Where is he? Does anyone see him? Please come forward! I'm sure he's here."

The public relations director was standing behind the last row of seats, directly behind a potted plant, trying to look as inconspicuous as possible.

"Well," continued the chairman, "if he's not here to take credit for it, perhaps it's not going to be that good after all. So, we'll see. Here goes."

JON. L. ALLEN

SLOW STARTER

A public relations manager for an oil company traveled frequently in South America, visiting exploration and production facilities. He was often accompanied by a Venezuelan freelance photographer with a limited command of English. Fortunately his conversational Spanish was good enough to converse with pilots and drivers along the way.

The trips weren't always a breeze. The public relations manager was an early riser, while the photographer preferred to stay out late in the evening and get up in mid-morning. Moreover, the photographer was inherently lazy and loath to start work until noon.

After the first several trips, the public relations manager came up with a surefire method for getting underway.

He started carrying his own camera with him. Whenever the pair arrived at a new site, he started taking pictures for future reference. More importantly, however, once he started, his Venezuelan photographer suddenly became energized and got to work.

Playing to his ego worked every time.

FIXED FOCUS

Cutting costs frequently has unexpected consequences, as all too many public relations executives can attest.

An editor for an oil company had such an experience when the company commissioned the building of two tankers in a European shipyard. He was told firmly he couldn't send his regular photographer from New York; it would be cheaper to send one from London. "Photographs are photographs," his boss reasoned. "So what's the difference?"

The photographer was assigned a reserved seat in the grandstand and shot dozens of frames from the same place. Obviously, they were virtually identical and of little use.

For the launching of the second vessel, the editor was able to arrange for his New York photographer to cover the event between assignments for other clients. The difference was nothing less then remarkable.

The editor's regular photographer had hired a boat to take him out in the harbor to cover low angles of the bow and stern. He'd climbed a crane at midday and shot the ship from above. He'd walked to the end of a jetty to photograph the tanker as it slipped into the water. He didn't even use the seat reserved for him in the grandstand.

The resulting photographs appeared in the company's magazine and annual report as well as in several petroleum, marine and international trade publications.

JON. L. ALLEN

FAST TRACK

At a multinational corporation, the post of assistant to the chairman was a prized assignment, invariably leading to greater responsibility. Young managers on the "fast track" rotated through the office every year.

The firm's public relations director consequently found himself repeating the same routine every year.

In addition to his other duties, he also served as secretary of the company's corporate contributions committee. Many appeals and invitations addressed to the chairman were signed by chairmen of other large companies. No matter who signed the letters, the return address and the suite number were often identical, that of a firm which handled dozens of similar projects each year—for a fee.

Whenever a new assistant moved into the chairman's office he was unaware of this and believed a personal response was called for every time. Moreover, the chairman and the public relations director met frequently to review the contributions budget, so the latter knew when a personal response was appropriate. Responsibility for everything else, the chairman delegated.

Over the course of a dozen years it was necessary to explain to as many assistants that, since they weren't privy to previous years' experience, each and every appeal was not new and most, in fact, were not in the budget.

LE

LOST IN TRANSLATION

A retired public relations executive recalls the importance of language skills when being considered for a new position. He lost out on an opportunity at a pharmaceutical company because, despite his fluent French and Spanish, he lacked a grasp of conversational German.

Finally, he was hired by a manufacturing firm just starting to stress the importance of its international operations. Both he and his wife were fluent in three languages.

After two years with the company, he still hadn't been sent to Europe or Latin America. He came up against reality.

"Well," his boss told him, "admittedly you know Europe very well and speak fluent French and you've traveled in South America and speak excellent Spanish. But we have three executives senior to you who've never been abroad, and they get to go first.

"No matter their trips will be totally unproductive and more costly than any you might take. Executive perks simply take precedence over real business."

CONSTRUCTION PROJECT

Within a few years of its construction, the new Air Force Academy quickly became the most popular tourist attraction in Colorado.

At a public affairs conference in Washington, D.C., the school's director of public affairs cited this pridefully, but bemoaned the fact that, unlike other popular tourist attractions, it lacked an adequate visitor center.

Later that day at the conclusion of the conference, the Air Force general who'd hosted the sessions summoned the public affairs director to the podium. He stepped back and pulled away a large blue cloth behind him to reveal a pegboard.

Wired to it were a hammer, saw, chisel, screwdriver, drill, pliers, tape measure, paint roller and other assorted hand tools.

"There you have it, a do-it-yourself visitor center kit," he smiled. "I know, given the right tools, you'll get the job done."

3-ALLE

EDITORIAL CONTACT

The wife of a public relations consultant in a small city makes every effort to help her husband secure new clients. At social functions especially, she goes out of her way to impress others with his expertise and contacts.

At a reception held at an art gallery one evening, the name of the editor of an important local magazine came up.

"My husband and Lee are very close friends," she offered. "They've known each other for years. I'm sure he'd be delighted to introduce him to you."

The corporate public relations executive to whom she was speaking was not the least bit impressed. He already knew the editor and knew Lee was not a "him" but an attractive and talented lady.

PRIVATE PRACTICE

Two plastic surgeons retained a public relations consultant to handle ground-breaking ceremonies for a new outpatient center.

Across the street from the site was a large hospital whose administrator was unhappy about the surgeons' plans. Fearful that patients would elect outpatient surgery because of its lower cost, he appealed to local officials to block construction of the center and deny it the necessary permits.

The public relations consultant, anticipating media interest in the controversy, met with his clients several times and drafted a detailed "position paper" to help them answer questions. When the day of the ground-breaking arrived, they were thoroughly prepared.

The ceremony proceeded without a problem. Television and newspaper reporters gathered around the surgeons at its conclusion. "What makes you think you can prevail against the hospital?" one of the reporters asked.

One of the surgeons answered the question, completely forgetting the facts in the "position paper."

"Because our lawyers are better than their lawyers."

The remark made the evening news roundup and the lead in an article in the local newspaper. The outpatient center eventually opened and was highly successful.

LE

CARIBBEAN CAPER

According to the public relations director of the American subsidiary of a leading European company, New Yorkers have a unique perspective and hear just what they want to hear, even though they speak the same language he does.

Several years ago, he had occasion to call his counterpart at a large industrial company and asked the telephone operator to connect him with someone "responsible for p.r."

The operator placed him on hold for several minutes. When she came back on the line, her response was a classic example of the barrier which divides those who speak the English language in different boroughs of New York.

"I'm sorry, we don't seem to have anyone here responsible for our Puerto Rican personnel," she informed him in a distinctive Brooklyn accent. "But I can connect you with someone in marketing who may be able to help you!"

SOUR NOTES

A seasoned public affairs professional with experience in business and government recalls some of his most absurd experiences happening during the time he served as a special assistant at the White House.

One of his favorites involved a lady who claimed she'd discovered the missing stanza of *America*, and insisted on presenting it to the President. Although he'd never heard of the fifth stanza, nor that it had been misplaced for 140 years, he agreed to accept it on behalf of the President.

On the appointed day, she was escorted to the Roosevelt Room where the special assistant and a photographer waited. When he asked her to hand him the sheet music, her eyes widened in surprise. She responded that no sheet music existed, but she planned to sing the stanza.

With the President working nearby in the Oval Office, a tactical retreat was essential. It was a pleasant day, so he suggested she sing the stanza on the lawn to enable the photographer to immortalize her with the White House in the background. She readily agreed.

She sang off-key and the photographer winced, but did his job. The special assistant found himself paying less attention to the words than the passersby who stopped to stare at the spectacle. "It must have been a sight," he recalls.

STICKY BUSINESS

In preparation for an interview with a financial editor, the president of a growing software company asked his public relations manager for some last-minute advice. Together, they went through a list of potential questions and appropriate answers. The public relations manager reviewed basic do's and don'ts. Most important, he cautioned, "If you don't want to see it in print, don't say it!"

The executive met with the reporter in late afternoon, handling a range of questions about the business and the company's relationships with various computer hardware firms. He told the public relations manager he believed the interview had been highly successful.

Two weeks later the article appeared. A direct quote attributed to the president was a comment that dealing with a very big computer company was "like swimming through a vat of peanut butter."

When the public relations manager asked how he could say such a thing, he responded, "I offered to drive him to the airport, then when he asked that question, I told him about the vat of peanut butter and we both laughed. I thought we were off the record after we left my office."

ADVANCE NOTIFICATION

It's not unusual to offer a newspaper or magazine an exclusive story, especially if the publication is influential or has an especially significant readership.

A press relations manager recalls, however, once delivering a single news release to a newspaper with a readership of less than 10,000, even though several hundred copies had been prepared.

His company planned to expand a nearby mining operation which produced a mineral for industrial customers. It was important to notify customers of the expansion, while not tipping off competitors. The local community would find out shortly anyway.

One week before the news release was delivered, the company's vice president of marketing sent confidential letters to customers, enclosing the "news" prior to the formal announcement.

The tactic was successful and numerous important customers expressed appreciation for the confidential letter.

Only weeks later did trade publications read by the company's competitors learn about the expansion. By then, the press relations manager could acknowledge the plans when queried. Meanwhile, the company had scored a customer relations advantage over its competitors.

RESEARCH AND DEVELOPMENT

A client insisted he and his public relations account executive fly to California together to gather material and scout photo possibilities for the annual report. They left Texas in the company's corporate jet, intending to visit several researchers under contract to the company. They'd no sooner landed than the account executive realized the client had neglected to reserve a rental car, nor made any hotel reservations. They settled for a motel in Sherman Oaks.

Since the client was a movie fan, he knew exactly how to make a night of it: cocktails on Rodeo Drive, a late dinner at Chasen's and nightcaps in the Polo Lounge at the Beverly Hills Hotel. At 4 a.m. they were back at the motel.

In the morning they visited a research project in Long Beach. It turned out to be a warehouse full of old movie props and an "engineer" with a severe hangover. The morning wasted, they headed for Malibu where the company was funding research on an innovative new energy source.

When photos were mentioned, the "scientist" in charge panicked. It turned out later he'd been spirited out of Germany after World War II and may have been living in Malibu under an assumed name.

That evening, the company jet rode a tailwind back to Texas. Elapsed time: 36 hours. Photo possibilities: None. Text: Less than 100 words (if lucky).

CALCULATED RESPONSE

A senior corporate executive had been invited to address a dinner meeting of a trade association in which he'd been active for many years. His public relations counsel helped him draft a speech with which he was pleased.

The public relations counsel also prepared a news release. It was a good story, making several important points. Copies were sent to 15 cities across the country in advance for release the evening of speech itself.

However, when the executive arrived at the dinner, he received a surprise. The invitation had been merely a ruse to get him there. The program was to be a tribute by colleagues and associates with whom he'd worked for many years.

As he listened to the speakers, he realized the news release was beyond recall. His public relations counsel was out on a limb with more then a few important editors.

After the tribute, he was summoned to the podium for a response. The speech was no longer appropriate. But as he reminisced about his career in the industry he wove each of the points in the news release into his remarks.

Later, his public relations counsel was impressed with his ingenuity, but more importantly, with his concern for the former's credibility when such a thought might not have occurred to many other executives.

-ALLE

CUSTOMER RELATIONS

An airline public relations representative once discovered it's possible to work for an organization for several years without even being aware of one's colleagues.

In his case, he was asked several times if he knew a particular colleague and had to admit he did not. He worked in the headquarters of an international airline in New York City, but was unable to find the name of his "colleague" in the company's personnel directory.

Eventually, he solved the mystery.

The individual in question turned out to be a suave, well-connected European who worked on the night shift at the airport when most international flights departed for Europe. His responsibilities included assisting first class passengers check in for their flights, escorting them to a private lounge and carrying their hand luggage to the departure gate. His role was unquestionably an important one, but his duties ranked considerably below those of the terminal's night supervisor.

He simply found it expedient to tell his elegant social acquaintances what he did was "public relations."

SOUND TRACK

The public relations director of a firm under contract to a government agency was handed a tough assignment several years ago. He was asked to develop a communications program directed at an Indian tribe in the Southwest which had no written language. The solution was to produce a film containing the story the agency wished to tell. Although the narration was written in English, a member of the tribe was enlisted to record it in the tribal language for transfer to the sound track.

It was an excellent film, he recalls, with several private screenings scheduled for key leaders at the tribe's regular inter-tribal ceremonial held in Arizona.

At the first showing, the film appeared to miss the audience completely. Members of the audience were walking out of the room. Several unkind comments were heard.

After a few minutes, the projectionist, also a member of the tribe, discovered the film had been wound improperly. It had been projected backwards, so the narration made no sense whatsoever — in any language!

Later screenings were more successful, much to the public relations director's relief. The tribal elders actually enjoyed the film and understood its message without further difficulty.

LE

QUESTION TIME

At the annual meeting of one of the largest corporations in Pittsburgh, an associate editor of a leading business magazine rose to ask a question. It was answered courteously, as she was a most attractive lady.

A few minutes later, she raised her hand again to ask another question, indicating she needed a microphone.

Slightly annoyed, the firm's corporate secretary summoned his public relations director.

"Tell her this is a shareholder meeting," he hissed, "not a press conference. She should sit down and shut up!"

When the public relations director conveyed the message, she replied, "But I am a shareholder."

The corporate secretary checked the lists before him. Much to his chagrin, he discovered she was indeed a shareholder in her own name and her holdings were much more than a mere odd lot. She owned a substantial number of shares, in fact considerably more than he owned himself. The public relations director couldn't restrain a grin.

The corporate secretary had just learned not every journalist is a starving busybody. Some might even have as much insight about his company as he did, and possess more shares than he might.

CAPITAL INVESTMENTS

Public relations writers who've worked as journalists take pride in their precise use of words. There are times, however, when some hyperbole is helpful.

A speech writer had this in mind while drafting a text for the chairman of a steel company. He referred to a "whopping" investment in a new automated mill.

When it was reviewed by a company lawyer, it came back with the word "substantial" substituted. "Whopping" was too colorful, the attorney explained. "Substantial" was more precise.

A few weeks later, the public relations writer was asked to review the text of a security analyst presentation. Twice on the same page it referred to expenditures as "substantial." In one instance, the reference was to expense for less than $100,000 for remodeling corporate offices. The second referred to a modernization program for several mills which exceeded $2 billion. The word "substantial" was obviously a favorite with the company's attorneys.

The lesson he learned is that in legalese "substantial" means anything from a few thousand to a few billion, while less "precise" words such as "whopping" are presumably reserved for the Federal deficit.

TALL STORY

The public relations director of a U.S. electronics firm prides himself on attention to detail.

Several years ago, his company planned a new factory in Southeast Asia, so he flew to Singapore several days ahead of his chief executive officer to complete arrangements for the formal announcement.

He wrote the chairman's speech, contacted government ministries, sent out invitations, prepared briefing kits for visiting executives, arranged gifts for those attending and inspected the hotel selected for the press conference.

His check-list, which he'd revised en route and again after his arrival in Singapore, had taken every conceivable detail into account.

However, he readily admits, there was one small item he overlooked. He'd failed to take into account the difference in height of podiums in Asia and California. When his chairman, who was 6'4", rose to speak, he couldn't see his text. It was no higher than waist level.

Luckily, the chairman was familiar with the text and able to take the situation in stride without having to read his remarks. And, adds the public relations director, nobody even noticed.

PRIDE OF AUTHORSHIP

Publication of a company's history is a major undertaking, but one in which those who do the most work invariably receive the least credit.

When a major manufacturing company published its history 20 years ago, authorship of the final text was entrusted to the company's most talented and polished writer. Predictably, he produced a superb manuscript.

Company management, however, refused to acknowledge his effort in the published volume.

Some months after publication, a company engineer was perplexed by a paragraph at the end of the final chapter, being one of the few readers who'd made it all the way through the book. While not incomprehensible, the paragraph seemed out of context, so he brought it to management's attention.

The paragraph was actually a puzzle. The first letter of every word, when combined, spelled out a complete sentence: "This book written by . . ."

LE

CLASS ACT

An international airline planned to inaugurate nonstop service from a West Coast city to Europe. Its public relations consultant arranged a tie-in with the city's powerful chamber of commerce. All the organization's top officers would be guests on the highly-publicized inaugural flight, everyone a successful businessman with an ego to match, and fully expected the airline to be especially efficient and solicitous of his needs. The group was accompanied by the chamber's own travel agent who had arranged the details.

However, all did not go as planned. Just as the guests on the flight were about to board the aircraft, a highly embarrassed airline official approached the public relations consultant and advised him there had been a mix-up with the boarding passes and it was too late to make a change.

There was no assurance any of the distinguished guests would be seated in first class or business class. Sure enough, after boarding, the chairman, president and other officers of the chamber of commerce found themselves seated in the middle of the coach section, four-abreast. The travel agent was comfortably seated by a window in the first class section.

For once in his career, the consultant was relieved not to be blamed for something beyond his control.

UNDER CONTROL

Due to the reputation it had built in a certain industry, a large public relations firm was retained by a leading company in that industry. The company's chairman liked the program, approved the budget and gave it his personal blessing.

"I assume you'll want to issue a news release to announce we're a new client?" he asked. The firm did and submitted it to the chairman for his approval.

The editor of a major trade publication who'd worked with both firms for many years used the release as the basis for a feature in which he said many positive things about the public relations agency's professionalism and role as a spokesman for the industry.

The new client telephoned a few days later. He was assured the news release had merely served as the basis for the feature, but the editor had drawn upon his own knowledge and experience to expand upon it. It was highly positive.

The client's next words came as a shock.

"You're fired!" he declared. "I hired you to control the news and you can't even control what's written about your own business."

Ten years later, the public relations firm's owner still wonders how many corporate executives believe publicists "control" the news. All too many, he surmises.

SIGN LANGUAGE

The public relations director of a manufacturing firm in a small Michigan city once learned how a small deed can yield surprising benefits.

When he was contacted by the local Thanksgiving Day parade committee for a sponsorship, he was distressed to find most of his annual budget had either been expended or was already committed.

He did have enough left for something modest. A float or a marching band were out of the question, but the price tag for signs which would be posted throughout the city announcing the time and route of the parade was reasonable.

He issued a check to the committee, which then arranged for the printing with due credit to his employer.

He was understandably surprised when he started receiving phone calls from employees and citizens thanking the company effusively.

As it turned out, some fast research revealed the printer who'd prepared the signs had misunderstood his instructions. Prominently displayed throughout the community every sign credited the company with sponsorship of the entire parade, not just a modest printing job.

COLLECTIVE BARGAIN

An Ohio public relations firm was retained by a freight handling company shortly after representing a coalition of labor unions. The president of the company was satisfied with the firm's work but somewhat uneasy about its previous connection with organized labor.

When freight handlers went out on strike, the president asked the firm to assist his bargaining team and was clearly anxious to see if they would cross the picket line.

One of the public relations firm's principals stopped at the picket line on his way to the first meeting. Angry pickets milled around, and the picket captain walked over to his car. Suddenly, the pickets turned their backs and waved him through. The company president never said a word about the incident, but was delighted when the union accepted his team's first wage and benefits offer several days later.

Weeks later over lunch, the president asked about it.

"It's a matter of trust," was the answer. "We already knew the picket captain and other union officers. Once they realized we were participating in the negotiations, they knew we'd only go along with a fair offer. We've built a reputation for being even-handed. The union respects that."

EXCESS BAGGAGE

For several weeks each year, the chairman and president of a company in the communications industry visited company locations with a "state of the company" presentation.

One year they asked their public relations director to prepare a pie-chart to show where company profits went. He turned the project over to a display house after providing guidance on layout, colors and text. It was a "rush" job.

The chart was ready on time and easily readable from a distance. Each piece of the pie was magnetized so it could be added as the presentation evolved.

There was only one problem. When the chart was taken apart and placed in its carrying case, it was almost seven feet in length and weighed close to one hundred pounds. Fortunately for the public relations director, his chairman and president were so pleased with it they never voiced a complaint.

However, they frequently kidded him mercilessly, pointing out that everywhere they went they needed an extra limousine for *his* chart and it was always necessary to leave one seat empty on their corporate jet for *his* chart. It was all good-natured teasing, however.

JON. L. ALLEN

PURE SCIENCE

There's no reason facts should stand in the way of a big news story. A couple of college teachers entered the premises of a nuclear power plant in the northeast illegally and took a small sample of its waste discharge. Then they called a local newspaper. It was a Friday afternoon.

The newsman was sure of the facts. The sample measured several million pico-curies, a highly toxic amount. The teachers' own suspicions were confirmed by an independent testing lab. The newsman made an effort to contact the plant's spokesman Friday evening, but time was running out.

His story ran over the weekend. It was very big. Copies were sent to the governor, members of the state legislature and Federal regulatory agencies.

It turned out the following week the small sample had been sent to the lab with no explanation. The technician who'd conducted the test had neglected to add a proper dilution factor in his calculations. The result was an error of three thousand to one.

The article hurt, even though the newspaper published a brief correction on page 22. The reporter was eventually promoted. The college teachers gained tenure within a few years. The power plant's public relations manager updated his resume and sought employment in another industry.

LEGAL EAGLE

A public relations executive was interviewed for a new public relations post at a large food processing firm.

An assistant general counsel conducted the interview, which included a plant tour, luncheon, and posing numerous questions about public relations, all of which were answered with candor. The interviewer assured the candidate he'd hear from the firm very soon.

Some weeks later the candidate learned from a friend that he too was in line for the job. He'd spent several hours with the lawyer over lunch, describing in detail every aspect of a proposed public relations program tailored to the company's needs. He'd been assured he would hear from the company very soon.

As it turned out, neither candidate ever heard from the firm again.

After a few months the first candidate learned from a friend in the same industry that the job had been filled. By whom? The assistant general counsel.

He's often wondered how many other candidates were "interviewed" to tap their expertise for the price of a few luncheons.

CURTAIN CALL

The publicist for a book publisher was among guests invited by an author to an elegant evening in his townhouse prior to publication of his new book. Because the book had a tie-in with a motion picture, the guest list included film and television producers and directors, investors and political figures.

The publicist bore a striking resemblance to an actor who'd just received glowing reviews for his performance in a Broadway play, so the author and other guests mistakenly assumed he was in "show business," and he was introduced to several other guests as his actor look-alike. The publicist didn't want to embarrass his host, so he played along and spent the evening trying to look appropriately modest.

The moment of truth came later, however, when he spotted the author chatting with his publisher. Again, he was eased into the conversation and introduced as his look-alike, to his considerable embarrassment.

Much to his credit, the publicist's boss, a regular theatergoer, didn't bat an eye. He leaned forward and lowered his voice.

"So that's why you're so tired when you come into work every morning," he quipped.

_E

BEST EFFORT

The chief executive officer of a leading hotel company was accustomed to entrusting his most important speechwriting assignments to his general counsel, an attorney he'd known since undergraduate days.

One time, the attorney came back in less than a week with a draft of remarks prepared for delivery to a trade association, fully expecting several revisions before it was completed.

After reading it, the chief executive officer rose and told him, "This is the best speech you've ever written for me. No changes needed!"

The general counsel, being honest, confessed he hadn't written it.

"To tell the truth," he explained, "last week I was tied up with some major litigation and simply didn't have the time. I asked our vice president for corporate communications to handle it. I'm sure he'll be delighted to learn how good you think it is."

Without hesitation, the chief executive officer handed it back to him. "On second thought," he responded, "I think it does need some revision."

PROFIT CENTER

The public relations manager of a diversified energy company has a favorite story he enjoys relating whenever his colleagues question his contributions to the "bottom line."

During the energy crisis in the early 1970's, he received a call one afternoon from the *Wall Street Journal* indicating the newspaper's London bureau had filed a story announcing that Britain's National Coal Board (NCB) had lifted its restrictions on coal imports. Because the public relations manager and the reporter were longtime friends, the latter hoped for a prompt comment.

The public relations manager called his counterpart in Pittsburgh immediately and within 20 minutes was able to respond that his firm's coal company was not only very interested, but that a senior executive would be on the evening flight to London with firm proposals for NCB to consider the following morning.

When competitors read the story in London and New York the next day, it was already too late. A press query, followed by a prompt response and swift action resulted in several million dollars in unanticipated new business, solely due to excellent press relations.

ON THE AIR

A Florida public relations counselor was asked at a seminar if he had a favorite "horror" story. He did.

Some 30 years ago, a client company introduced a new product and dispatched a company aircraft around the country with several key executives on board. His assignment was to set up radio interviews throughout Florida.

His task was made all the easier when he realized one of the company's executives was the son of a radio comedian whose show had been heard during the golden age of radio in virtually every living room in America. Stations loved the idea, and a full schedule was soon booked statewide.

When the group arrived in Florida, the counselor proudly showed them the line-up.

"My God," the company's public relations director exclaimed. "Didn't anyone tell you?"

"Tell me what?"

"He has a severe speech impediment. He stutters badly."

Thanks to a glib sales manager traveling with the group, the counselor found a way to overcome the problem.

Every time an interviewer suggested the executive must have many wonderful memories of the golden age of radio, the sales manager jumped into the conversation.

"He certainly does. He told us a terrific story at dinner last night." Then he'd proceed to relate the story.

MANAGEMENT OBJECTIVES

Contacted by an executive recruiter, a public relations manager flew to an interview in a distant city with a firm created by the merger of two companies in the same industry.

He learned from some fellow professionals he was being considered to replace a competent public relations director unaware he'd soon be out of a job. That was disquieting.

When he met with the president of the firm, he asked for a job description and a corporate mission statement. "I'm embarrassed, but we don't have any," was the response. He and the company president then spent almost an hour outlining a corporate public relations plan on paper.

When the chief executive officer entered the room, he offered the candidate the job at an excellent salary without discussion. When shown the proposed plan, he dismissed it at a glance. "We'll figure out what you're supposed to do after you're on the job." That, too, was disquieting.

The candidate, who liked his current job, concluded he'd received more than enough warning signals. He told the incredulous chairman of the board the offer wasn't worth his consideration. Not only did the company have any sense of mission, but also no idea what his duties might entail. He also didn't relish the prospect of wondering every day if his successor was being interviewed in similar circumstances without his knowledge.

HIGHER AUTHORITY

When an auto parts plant in central Pennsylvania was ready to celebrate its 20th anniversary, a local public relations consultant called the plant manager to schedule an interview. He'd been assigned to write an article for a regional business publication.

"I'd be delighted to spend some time with you," the plant manager responded. "But you have to get approval from our corporate headquarters in Detroit." He provided the name and phone number of the appropriate division public relations contact.

The writer's call to Detroit was brief. His contact granted permission immediately, even though he was unfamiliar with the publication.

The public relations consultant called the plant manager to schedule the interview. He wasn't in his office, but his secretary selected a date and time for the visit.

"I'm sorry you had to call Detroit," she apologized. "But it's company policy. They have so many highly-paid people on staff there, I suppose they have to give them something to do."

JON. L. ALLEN

UPS AND DOWNS

Sometimes company managements have an unfortunate tendency to place unqualified people in public relations posts, especially if no other assignment is available.

One such individual, two years short of retirement, was placed in a top corporate position a few months before his company announced its relocation to another city. It was a big story in the other city, and a leading newspaper sent a reporter to file background stories.

The reporter set a date to interview the new public relations executive, but the latter "stonewalled" throughout the interview, refused to acknowledge even the most trivial facts and arranged for his secretary to cut the interview short with a summons from "upstairs," i.e. the men's room.

"Well, I guess I showed that little jerk," he exulted after the reporter had left. The experienced professionals on his staff winced at his insensitivity and rudeness.

The reporter spent the following hour riding elevators in the company's headquarters, chatting with employees and produced two articles about the relocation, each filled with quotes reflecting their feelings.

When clippings of his stories arrived, the department head was furious. "I didn't tell him that. How dare he use unauthorized anonymous comments?" Fortunately, the relocation also resulted in his early retirement.

ARCHIVAL QUALITY

A multinational corporation had contributed generously to an archaeological restoration in Southeast Asia. When it was finished, an article in the company's slick, external magazine was scheduled, illustrated with several recent color photos.

The magazine's editor also thought it appropriate to use a photo taken many years earlier to illustrate the "before" and "after" of the restoration. Fortunately, he was able to find a satisfactory photo in the company's archives taken more than 20 years earlier. Although it had faded and the colors were washed out, the expense of restoring it was worth it since it enhanced the layout.

A few weeks after publication, he received a bill for several hundred dollars from a freelance photographer of whom he'd never heard. Neither had any of his colleagues. The photographer had apparently taken the original photo many years earlier, but anyone who'd ever dealt with him had long since retired.

The editor checked the mailing list for the magazine and found the photographer's name on it. He approved the bill for payment, of course, but removed the name from the mailing list and never heard from the photographer again. He never cared much for surprises.

JON. L. ALLEN

WINNERS AND LOSERS

Each year, the weekend prior to the industry's major annual convention, a major oil company always held an outing for sports-minded editors and reporters who covered the energy beat. Several senior executives from the company's headquarters were invited to accompany the group.

When the convention was held in Houston one year, the company chartered a fishing boat at Port Isabel on South Padre Island for a day of angling for red snapper in the Gulf of Mexico.

One wire service reporter organized a pool to which every angler contributed ten dollars. It would go to whoever caught the largest fish of the day.

The company's press relations manager, a reluctant fisherman, had the misfortune to catch not only the first fish of the day and the most fish of the day, but also the largest fish of the day! A paper bag full of cash was pressed into his hands when the boat reached the dock. He didn't need instructions on what to do.

That evening, after dinner when everyone adjourned to the hospitality suite, it proved a real test of his skill to lose it all back and more during some serious poker.

LE

GOOD SHOW

One of the major public relations firms in the Middle West had been invited to make a presentation to a leading trade association. The committee which heard the presentation was comprised of 15 representatives of the largest companies in the industry.

The presentation was pure "show business," with multiple slide and film projectors, dimmers, a taped soundtrack and spotlights on each speaker. As it built to a climax, members of the agency group smiled at each other confidently.

When it concluded and the lights were turned on in the room, one of the members of the selection committee rose to comment.

"That was very impressive." he said. "In fact, I was impressed the last time I sat through it as a member of the selection committee for another trade association of which my company is a member."

"It only lacks one thing," he concluded. "Originality." The account was awarded to another firm.

FRIENDLY RIVALS

The public relations manager for a division of a large auto maker visited New York frequently to meet with magazine and newspaper editors. On one occasion, he found himself in the city at the same time as his counterpart for a major competitor.

Despite the fact they were friendly rivals, they'd also been neighbors in Michigan for more than a decade, so they agreed to co-host a luncheon with the editor of a popular magazine interested in automotive innovations.

As it happened, the luncheon conversation turned from business to personal matters, and the manager's competitor mentioned his rival's recent house fire and his interest in remodeling and restoration.

Coincidentally, the editor's magazine also carried articles on these subjects and he immediately commissioned a freelance article. Subsequently, the public relations manager contributed several cover stories and articles to the magazine, developing a second career as a freelancer.

He still can't recall if either he or his rival were successful in placing stories about their respective employers' products. But, they both recalled the occasion with amusement in later years and agreed that media relations specialists have a lot in common with literary agents!

PATHS OF GLORY

A story an acknowledged leader in the public relations profession tells on himself started with a phone call from a corporate executive he'd known for many years.

His caller, vice president of advertising and public relations for one of the nation's largest consumer product companies, inquired if he'd be in New York on a certain day and free for lunch.

After hanging up, he rushed into his partner's office to tell him about he luncheon. "Do you think we have a chance on the account?" he asked.

"Wouldn't that be something!" was the reply. The account would be bigger than any they'd ever had.

Following the luncheon, he returned to his office the next day and reported to his partner. His mixture of elation and disappointment obviously showed.

Unfortunately, he hadn't been offered an opportunity to make a proposal for the account. He'd been asked if he'd be willing to be nominated for a term in the prestigious position of president of a premier professional society.

His partner naturally felt let-down. But, he himself looked back later upon the year he served in the post as one of his most memorable experiences, more rewarding personally than having gained a new, albeit very large, account.

HEAD COUNT

Public relations practitioners invariably have to explain to colleagues and clients many times that newspaper reporters write stories, while desk-bound editors write headlines appropriate to the length and importance of the stories and decide where they will appear on each page.

Many find it useful to place a headline above the text of a news release. It not only alerts an editor to the subject of release, but it often expresses it succinctly enough to make the headline writer's task easier.

One counselor who moved to Alaska some years ago had a unique experience unlike any he'd had before. He'd sent out a routine news release about a client company's plans to open a new office. He placed a brief headline above the text and included the name of the new manager who would head the office.

Much to his surprise, he received a call from a local business editor at a daily newspaper asking quite seriously if he could modify the headline slightly so it would fit the following day's news hole.

Of course, he readily agreed, and the story ran verbatim the following day. It was the first time he'd ever been asked to agree to such a change, but not the last, as he learned Alaskan editors unlike their colleagues elsewhere tend to be surprisingly accommodating.

LE

MORAL DILEMMA

A public relations staffer at a small company faced a moral dilemma when asked by a senior executive to do something he believed violated his professional code of ethics. The firm, a chemical specialties company, produced a product formulated differently than those of several competitors who had discontinued the line.

The staffer was told to telephone editors at leading trade publications and draw attention to the competitors' problems. He was told to point out that his company was the only reliable source for the product; in making the phone calls, he was cautioned to explain that everything was "off the record," for "background only."

Unwilling to undertake the assignment, he discussed its ethical implications with the firm's chief executive. The latter was supportive and told him not to make the calls. He assured the staffer that he'd discuss it with the senior executive.

Some months later, when the public relations staffer was applying for unemployment benefits, the benefits counselor telephoned his former employer in his presence.

He observed that the counselor made a notation on his application that one reason for leaving the company had been "unable to follow instructions."

TEMPERATURE RISING

No matter how carefully one plans for a special event, a Georgia public relations consultant is convinced one can't anticipate every circumstance.

Some years ago his firm staged a grand opening for a branch bank in a small town. Civic leaders predicted less than 200 people would show up on a cold February day.

Among the free refreshments were cookies, of which 50 dozen were ordered from a local bakery. The promotion was a great success. Close to 1,000 people turned out. The cookies lasted less than an hour, making it necessary to buy more from every grocery store in town. He'd learned a lesson.

The next branch opening, in a larger town, was set for mid-May. This time almost 2,000 people was a realistic expectation. The bakery delivered 500 dozen cookies.

It was an unseasonably hot afternoon and the visitors consumed immense quantities of cold drinks. But they ate few cookies. At the end of the day several hundred remained.

The consultant concluded the only thing to do was make the best of the situation and gain some goodwill. The remaining cookies were delivered to orphanages, nursing homes, a boys' club, and the YMCA and YWCA. He'd learned another lesson.

COLLEGE TRY

Even communications professionals can make a mistake once or twice. How about three times in a row?

When a leading Midwestern university realized it had over a thousand graduates in central Indiana, plans were made to organize a local chapter of the alumni association. A public relations educator and his wife co-chaired a local committee which made arrangements for the first meeting to be held at a well-known restaurant in Indianapolis.

The university's alumni relations office mailed the announcements. The first mistake was placing a map of the location for the event on the reverse of the reply card. Everyone who sent in a response also returned a map.

To rectify the error, the alumni relations office sent a letter to all respondents, reminding them of the time and place of the event. Unfortunately, the map which was enclosed depicted a completely different location.

Finally, the meeting was held with a slightly lower attendance then anticipated.

Then, the public relations educator adds, came the third mistake. Proud to recognize the formation of new alumni chapter in the heart of the Hoosier State, the university sent a large banner to be unfurled at the meeting. It was fine, except for one thing. Indianapolis was misspelled.

HEALTHY COMPETITION

Thirty years ago, before newspapers intercepted visitors with security guards and receptionists, public relations practitioners had ready access to the newsroom

An airline public relations executive recalls an occasion when the merger of two major airlines was announced. He went to the fourth floor of the *New York Times* to deliver a joint news release to the business desk.

As he crossed the newsroom, a reporter on the newspaper's transportation desk looked up and spotted him. He was on his feet immediately, sensing a story. He and the public relations executive arrived at the business news section simultaneously.

When the executive returned to his office, his boss asked what the reaction had been in the newsroom.

"They were fighting over it when I left," he replied. "Each of them wants the story for his section. They were going to ask the night managing editor for a decision."

Fortunately, both airlines were headquartered in New York and their chief executive officers were colorful personalities. Neither section prevailed. The story ran on page one and jumped inside the first section, accompanied by charts explaining the scope of the merger.

E

THE RIGHT STUFF

As the chairman of a large public relations firm found himself busier and busier, he needed larger and larger briefcases. Sometimes, he had to make several presentations to potential clients on the same day without an opportunity to return to his office.

As he prepared to make a presentation in midtown Manhattan one afternoon, he pulled a set of printed and bound proposals from his briefcase and distributed them to his audience.

"There seems to be a problem," the chief executive officer of the company exclaimed. "I believe you've given us the wrong proposal. Here, look at this."

The public relations executive would have welcomed a natural disaster at that moment. The folders he'd handed out were leftover copies prepared for a presentation he'd made earlier in the day a few blocks away.

He retrieved them and distributed another set of the right ones. Although his presentation was first-rate, he's always wondered if his gaffe was responsible for another firm securing the account.

MODEL RELEASE

Rarely, if ever, does a public relations executive have an opportunity to include a photograph of his spouse on the cover of his company's annual report. Just such happened, however, several years ago when a multinational corporation selected the theme for its annual report.

Rather than depict company facilities or products, it was decided to emphasize international operations. A montage of color photographs with an international flavor was requested.

The final layout consisted of photographs of well-known scenes in Australia, Kenya, Thailand, Egypt and Pakistan.

After much research by the designer, the best color shot for Japan turned out to be one of the impressive gateway to the Meiji Shrine in Tokyo. It was one of several transparencies the public relations manager had taken himself while on a business trip to Japan several months earlier. Among the figures in the middle distance was an American lady with red hair and a tan raincoat who never stopped walking as he composed his photographs.

The company's executive committee was delighted with the annual report. Only the public relations manager's closest friends, however, spotted his wife in the heart of Tokyo.

-ALLE

BORN LEADER

For 18 years a Chicago public relations firm toiled for a consumer products company, helping move it from obscurity to a position of leadership in its industry and making its chairman a nationally-recognized business leader.

Over the years, dozens of articles had been published. The chairman had been interviewed on every network and numerous local talk shows.

A flamboyant person, he took great joy in never acknowledging he'd attained national prominence as a result of a creative, sustained public relations effort.

One particular day, his public relations counsel entered his office and found him glowing with pride. A leading newsmagazine was planning to profile him in an upcoming issue and had contacted him directly.

Aware of his client's unusual personality, the public relations counsel inquired discreetly, "How did they happen to think of you?" The chairman chose to ignore the question, obviously still pleased with himself.

The public relations counsel recalls he'd simply chosen to disregard the thousands of lines published about him and his company and the many hours of radio and television time arranged for him for almost two decades.

"Nevertheless, he was a fascinating man."

SURPRISE PACKAGE

Some public relations firms publish media directories which fellow professionals find useful. Most are regional, statewide or local in scope.

One year, a firm placed a routine order for a media guide published by another firm in the same state. It arrived securely wrapped for shipping.

Upon opening it, one of the principals in the firm discovered why the package was unusually thick. The volume had been encased in several layers of computer paper.

The paper wasn't new, however. It had been used. The partner unfolded it to read the text.

Much to his surprise, what he was reading was his competitor's financial statement, client billings and other proprietary information for the previous year. He held a complete picture of the other firm's business in his hands.

The mailroom which had packed the book may have been loath to let all that paper go to waste, but the partner was sure management would have made a modest investment in a document shredder if they'd known what happened.

GOOD WORD

Most corporate public relations departments maintain several shelves of reference books, as they usually deemed to be most competent at answering management queries.

This was very apparent to one public relations director who worked for a chief executive officer with a restless curiosity. Whenever he had a question, he'd ask his secretary to find the answer, then during the morning he'd ask his executive assistant and the company's chief economist the same question. At least one of them would call the company librarian.

Invariably, the public relations director would receive at least three calls, posing the same question, but, of course, never revealing it had originated with the chairman. Why would any of the callers want to share credit for finding the answer?

The public relations director had a favorite story about one such call.

One morning, during a board meeting, a question came up. The answer, it seemed, might be found in the Bible. The chairman's executive assistant called the public relations director.

"Does your department have a Bible?" he inquired.

"Yes, we have two," the public relations director responded. "But they're both in use right now."

STANDING ROOM ONLY

When modern medicine first made it possible to change one's gender with surgery, it naturally attracted media attention. Several beneficiaries of the procedure became minor celebrities.

Celebrities, of course, need public relations counsel to help them through public appearances and interviews, so one such recipient of an operation who had authored a book retained a seasoned theatrical and television publicist with a reputation for details.

Prior to his/her public appearance at a New York hotel, a friend of the client's publicist stopped to chat with her while the celebrity author was in the ladies' room.

When her client emerged, the publicist excused herself and dashed into the ladies' room.

She was out again almost immediately, a self-satisfied grin on her face.

"The toilet seat was *up!*" she exclaimed. In addition to paying attention to details, she verified facts firsthand.

CUTTING EDGE

The tools of the public affairs profession vary with every situation. In one instance, they were as ordinary as a couple of pairs of scissors.

Members of the armed forces have long been regular readers of the weekly *Army Times*, *Navy Times* and *Air Force Times*. During the years when major bases fielded intramural sports teams, the last of these publications sponsored an annual all-Air Force football team.

Two enterprising young public affairs officers at a base well below the Mason-Dixon Line set out to beat the system. They spent several Saturday mornings at the publication's local distributor clipping write-in ballots from copies which had been returned unsold.

These were then distributed to the commanders of the base's security police, food service, transportation and maintenance squadrons with instructions to have their men cast votes for whomever they wished as long as they nominated the team's quarterback, a former college standout, now a junior base engineer, for that position.

Of course, he won. He was flown to Washington for an awards banquet and presented with a gold watch. He never knew, of course, the award he received was due less to his athletic ability, than to two pairs of sharp scissors.

JON. L. ALLEN

WHAT'S IN A NAME

Two public relations professionals met frequently for lunch at the Overseas Press Club in New York City. One was responsible for media relations for a Fortune 500 company. The other was the owner of his own consulting firm.

One day, the latter had a problem. One of his clients was assembling a multi-industry conglomerate consisting of companies in unrelated industries: magazine publishing, food and beverages, cosmetics and car rentals. The consultant was working with firms with experience in creating new corporate identities and had been asked to recommend a name for the new corporation.

His luncheon companion was familiar with the client's reputation as a businessman and art collector who also built a museum in California to house his treasures. He was also cognizant of the client's outsized ego.

"Why doesn't he simply name the company for himself?" he suggested.

Several weeks later, he learned that's exactly what transpired. The chief executive officer of the conglomerate had spent thousands of dollars, but the name of his new firm, derived from a casual remark, was compensated only by the consultant picking up that day's luncheon check.

LANGUAGE BARRIER

When a multinational energy company awarded a contact for a large project in Spain, the company's chief executive officer decided a formal announcement and news release were necessary.

The firm's vice president of advertising and public relations, a former salesman, took charge of the situation since there was a tight deadline.

He assigned a junior member of his staff to draft the news release, which was promptly approved. The next hurdle was to arrange for a Spanish translation.

Since the firm's corporate headquarters in New York City was only a few blocks from the United Nations, finding a translator was easy.

However, feedback from Madrid when the news releases were delivered was negative, critical and sarcastic. The United Nations translator had not been a Spaniard, but from Venezuela. His rendering was an embarrassment to his client, its representative in Madrid and members of the Spanish business press.